THE SOUTHERN WAY

CONTENTS

© Kevin Robertson (Noodle Books) and the various contributors 2011
ISBN 978-1-906419-53-0
First published in 2011 by Kevin Robertson
under the **NOODLE BOOKS** imprint
PO Box 279
Corhampton
SOUTHAMPTON
SO32 3Z
www.noodlebooks.co.uk
editorial@thesouthernway.co.uk
Printed in England by
Ian Allan Printing Ltd
Hersham, Surrey

"JACK" THE RAILWAY DOG.

Opposite page - Bude station with Class M7 No 252 departing on its sedate journey to Halwill sometime after its high speed exploits of the Exeter-Plymouth main line. No 252 was a member of the first batch of the M7 class constructed at Nine Elms in June 1897. This batch was initially to be built as part of the Adams T1 class (Nos 368-77) which was cancelled by the LSWR board to be replace by a new design of 'large passenger bogie tanks' of Drummond design. The South Western called for tenders 20 locomotives, expecting a price of around £1,600. The lowest tender was that offered by Robert Stephenson & Co and exceeded the board's estimate by some £790. To reduce the unit cost the batch was increased to 25 and the work transferred to the LSWR's own works at Nine Elms. The 25 entered service between February and December 1897 costing £1,580 each. Carrying numbers 242-56 and 667-76, this batch was to remain intact until July 1957 when No 250 was withdrawn, the last, No 254, going in May 1964. As built the batch sported identifying features such as short front platform and combined leading splashers and sandboxes. The M7s were scattered all over the LSWR network, No 252 was allocated to Exmouth Junction for service over the lines of Devon and Cornwall, and amongst others being used on the semi-fast Exeter-Plymouth services. It was while on such a service on 6 March 1898 that No 252 came to grief when, running chimney first, it left the track two miles north of Tavistock and came to rest parted from its train after running along the ballast for 220 yards. As a result of the Board of Trade inspection the class was restricted to suburban services and those not demanding periods of high speed running. By March 1906 No 252 was working the London suburban services being shedded at Strawberry Hill. Much of the suburban network was electrified in the early 20th century and its extension to Strawberry Hill, Hounslow loop, along with the Hampton Court and Shepperton branches saw a significant reduction in the numbers of steam locomotives required. Although not initially fitted, No 252 was fitted with cable-control motor-train equipment to provide a pool of locomotives to cover routine maintenance and works visits. Following the Grouping No 252 received Maunsell green livery in March 1924 and carried an E prefix to its number, the latter being removed in September 1931, during which year it was transferred from Strawberry Hill to Nine Elms where it was to remain until 1937 when a return to the West Country was made, therefore dating the image to just before World War 2. It was one of three engines sub-shedded by Exmouth Junction, the others being 320 and 668, covering two duties on the Bude-Halwill line. Upon Nationalisation No 252 was to be found shedded at Exmouth Junction before a move to Barnstaple was made in 1951 having received its BR number 30252 and lined black livery in January 1950. No 30252 was withdrawn early in February 1959, by which time the M7s had been usurped in the West Country by the Ivatt Class 2MTs, BR Class 3MTs and diesel multiple-units. No 30252 did not survive the torch that long as it was cut up at Eastleigh later the same month. (Contributed.)
Further reading: LSWR Locomotives: The Drummond Classes, D. L. Bradley, Wild Swan Publications 1986. The Book of the M7s, Peter Swift, Irwell Press, 2010.

Editorial Introduction

I have to admit to a slight amount of trepidation in what follows as I am going to freely admit what I am sure several already suspected, when starting a new issue I am never exactly sure where each issue of 'Southern Way' is going to lead!

I mention this as whilst there is of course a plan relative to the main articles, it is often the fillers (no less important) that are the problem. Does one follow a theme to try and achieve a balance between companies, subjects, areas etc, or should it be an attempt to respond to present interest and themes? This might even require a bit of elaboration as it might appear strange that notwithstanding our subject matter having ceased to exist decades earlier, by attempting to listen to the grapevine it is clear that specific topics fall in and out of favour, corresponding sometimes with a new release from the model market.

Only a few years ago there was little that had been covered in both book and model form and consequently with the mainstream subjects now reaching saturation point many have turned their attention to the lesser known, peripheral, aspects of the interest and hobby. One of these is Permanent Way, so whilst I was slightly unsure when Graham Hatton suggested a second tranche on Paddock Wood, I have to admit what he has produced is I believe even more interesting than the first time around.

It is fascinating to learn of the tricks of the trade in Graham's notes, as well as the pitfalls (and local penalties) metered out to the men on the ground should they fail to deliver at the time. Sitting in a comfortable warm office at the time of preparing this piece for inclusion makes me realise just how lucky I am and how true it was that permanent way staff had the hardest jobs of all on the railway.

I am also wary about passing comment on a particular article lest it appear I have a specific favourite, but I will admit there is one this month that has somehow struck a particular chord. This is Ben Brooksbank's piece - well Part 1A of the full version - relating to his train observations in the period 1939 to 1947. To actually learn what was running and the types of trains and working during this time is a revelation. We can be so glad the censor did not get to work and confiscate what today is not just a valuable record, but one, because of its diversity and detail, may well be unique. (Having naturally had a preview of what there is to follow, I can promise the next instalment is just as revealing.) It is not just the numbers either that are fascinating - to learn what was actually involved in travelling during those years is enthralling - but it is also Ben's hints at life during this difficult period as well. Having had the privilege of meeting him several times I suspect there is more than a degree of modesty involved. With Ben's knowledge and consent, I have also taken the unusual step (for space reasons) of splitting Part 1 between this issue and 'Wartime Southern Part 3'.)

As I have stated before, the purpose of 'SW' has always been to try and bring out the detail behind the railway, both human and factual, as well as affording an outlet for additional information to complement an already published piece. I have always been perfectly happy to cross boundaries here, in this way, just as in human nature, there are some who are easy to get on with and others less so, however, at the end of the day it is the information that matters.

I feel I am starting to duplicate a theme stated previously, so also to make up for a somewhat elongated diatribe on the last occasion, this time I am deliberately keeping things shorter.

What I will conclude with is that I am delighted to present another enlarged issue. Do not be fooled though, we will be reverting to the more usual 100 pages shortly. Extra pages are only possible dependent upon certain factors, the principal one being that each issue has to fit in to a set costing, print and reproduction. Anyway, assuming a few cold days in spring - it was certainly cold when I was writing this in December, I hope the extra items may afford a means to pass the time.

As ever, thanks to all, readers and contributors, as well as throwers of brickbats and plaudits for your continuing support.

Kevin Robertson

editorial@thesouthernway.co.uk

Front cover - Eeking out its last days in revenue earning service, 'L' class 4-4-0 No. 31760 engages in a spot of shunting at Aldershot.
Roger Thornton / KR Collection

Pages 2 and 3 - Those who have persevered (I do hope the word is not suffered) 'Southern Way' since near the start, will recall the image of Grove Road, Deptford that appeared in Issue No. 1. No excuses then for the inclusion of this second scene, this time of 'D1' No. 255. I suspect it is the presence of the people, the man unconcerned, the woman clearly attracted by the noise of the train, the date is not recorded. The image was loaned to us consequent upon a visit to regular reader, Les Burberry. In conversation about a totally unrelated topic, Les announced, "There is an album on the table that might interest you as well....". The result, one of several wonderful images that will appear in due course.

Opposite top - Recently submitted by Bob Winkworth was this delightful 'Stuart' card, the reverse is dated 22 January 1905.

Above - I first met Ray Bartlett when, as a driver, he would often come and take his break mid-shift in the Plan Arch at Waterloo. Here he would regale the likes of Reg Randall, George Reeve, Roger Simmonds and myself with questions and comments about whatever happened to be our topic of discussion on that day. Meeting Ray again recently, he provided the attached view of Bude, very similar to those seen on page 20/21 of Issue 6.

Rear cover - No 34092, 'City of Wells' hurrying west at Clapham Junction on 2 June 1964.
Richard Bairstow

Two members of the L.B. Billinton LB&SC B4X class displaying Southern livery and in their last years of operation. Above is No. 2052 entering Farnborough on 8 July 1950 working a Special from Waterloo in connection with the 1950 Air Display. Below, No. 2072 is recorded at Brighton on 18 December 1949.

(All photographs accompanying this article by the Author.)

We have been privileged to have been passed several notes of observations and spottings over the years: the sort fondly recalled as having greasy thumbprints, rusty staples and illegible notes accompanying certain numbers.

None though are as comprehensive as the record kept by Ben Brooksbank. A retired professional, Ben has made a study of certain aspects of railways, notably WW2, some of his notes on this subject having appeared in his superb 'LONDON MAIN LINE WAR DAMAGE' (Capital Transport). His fastidiousness for detail make his compilations unique.

It is both a pleasure and a privilege to record some of Ben's SR notes here.

References to footnotes will be found at the end of the section on page 16.

WATCHING TRAINS ON THE SOUTHERN 1938 - 1948

Part 1A: Prior to and During World War Two

Ben W. L. Brooksbank

Life is difficult and one of the most trying times is adolescence. Adolescence is when you have to come to terms with the dreadful reality that the world does not revolve around you: there are other people out there whose needs and desires are just as important as yours. You are presented with the great challenges of starting to fend for yourself and to compete and cooperate with – and put up with – other young people. Girls possibly find adolescence somewhat easier than do boys: females are programmed to be more cooperative and caring than are males; males are programmed to work with tools and machines and to compete with other males -- cooperation is a skill they have to learn. Aside from these differences, which come to the fore in adolescent humans, there are basic personality traits that differ between human individuals. One of the most fundamental and pervasive of human traits is revealed by what is known as the extraversion/introversion dimension: as with the gender differences, most of us are aware of this characteristic – at least in other people if not in themselves!

These psychological factors, modified by technological and social conditions in Western countries – Britain in particular – in the mid-20th century, underlay the pastime of Train Spotting in the days of my youth. Boys beginning adolescence want to get away from home (between meals!) and 'do their own thing'[(1)]. The extraverts created the gangs, while the introverts either strung along because they were made afraid of being introverts by the extraverts, or else they had the courage to do it on their own, perhaps with other male introverts.

The psychobiological programming of males to make tools leads them to love machines: the bigger and noisier the machine the better. In the 19th century they invented the steam locomotive. It supplanted the horse as a powerful tool, for transport and other purposes and moreover it almost seemed to be 'alive'. However, except for the privileged few who aspired to become Engine-Drivers, the sense of power transferred to the locomotive had to be vicarious; it needed the advent of the motor car and the lorry really to substitute psychologically for the horse. Indirectly, it was no doubt the availability to adolescent and young men in the second half of the 20th century of first the motor-bike, then the car and the lorry, which caused the gangs of train-spotters to disappear. Nevertheless, you do see a few train-spotters nowadays, but they are adult and not in gangs.

Train-spotting was a pursuit for teenagers that was harmless -- and badly needs a modern substitute, but it exhibited other important psychological traits. Important to all males is competition -- the drive to do better than the others. Another motivation, shown by young male introverts in particular, is the desire to put order and sense into things, to make lists. This is allied to the -- usually masculine -- desire to understand how activities (like railway systems) are organised, and how things – machines, or anything – work. So we make lists of engine-numbers, note down the ones we see and try to beat the other boys with our collection of 'cops'. If we are a little more advanced, we go on to study the organisation behind the traffic movements and we study timetables and note down when and where we saw the engine and what train it was working. This is what I myself did; I also wanted to preserve my 'lovely engines', so I photographed them.

I began photography at Christmas 1945, but inevitably with a primitive old (second-hand) camera, which would not 'stop' moving trains: only two years later was I given one that could (a Kodak Retina, second-hand). The other problem was -- in those 'halcyon' days (for Train-Watchers) just after the War – film was in very short supply. I was constantly chasing round shops of all kinds in Central London asking "Have you got any film in yet?", although eventually a cousin in RAF Photoreconnaissance secured for me a whole roll of surplus 35 mm film. By 1955 my Kodak Retina was packing up and I could not afford to replace it, so most of my photographs in those later 'halcyon days' were pretty useless. Late in 1956 I got a fairly decent new camera, also a competent and helpful work colleague who did my developing-and-printing, then many of my railway photographs turned out well. Still, half a century later, I cherish my pictures – and only wish I had more[(2)]! Moreover, to my surprise, I find that grown men too young to have ever known the Railways or the Steam Locomotive in the mid-20th century, can be really interested in what I saw back in those days. In my young days, you were taken as rather a crank if you 'wasted' good film taking photographs of those 'dreary and dirty old steam trains'.

I started noting down 'engine-numbers' in 1936, when I was nine years old, but the first year I began to note locations or workings was 1938, when I discovered the joys of Watching Trains at their busiest, on Summer Saturdays. I have to admit, nevertheless, that I found the Southern Railway the least fascinating of the Big Four. Living in London (from age 18) I was able to watch trains as well on the GWR, LMS and LNER. I spent relatively little time beside the SR, because to a great extent there was 'nothing but juice-boxes' to watch, which all looked the same and had no 'personality'. Also, I was unusual during the War in having for a teenager the necessity to travel about the country quite a lot – and young enough not to be taken to be a spy by the staff or other passengers who saw me so assiduously noting down all the trains as they passed [3].

On the SR, the earliest notes I made that are at all meaningful date from September 1938, when during a holiday at Lee-on-the-Solent [4] I made notes – of sorts.

The first 'Log' *(Table 1)* was on **4 September 1938**-- a Sunday of all days – at **Fareham**, times not recorded but I must have been there for several hours:-

TABLE 1: Fareham, 4 September 1938			
Class	Number	Working	Notes
D15	466	Bournemouth – Margate EP	A remarkable through train!
T9	713	Margate – Bournemouth EP	Ditto
M7	480	Eastleigh – Gosport OP	Returned later
T9	122	LE, then OP to Portsmouth	
T9	114	Salisbury – Portsmouth OP	
T9 + L11	288 + 417	Plymouth – Brighton EP	288 came off at Fareham
T9	702	? – Portsmouth OP	
L12	429	Portsmouth – Bournemouth EP	
S11	400	To 'Waterloo via Alton'	That it went beyond Alton seems unlikely
K10	150	Portsmouth – Salisbury OP	
T9; S11; D15	118, 708; 399; 471	Not recorded	

On Wednesday **7 September** I recorded the following at **Fareham** *(Table 2)* in about 3½ hours from 13.30:-

TABLE 2: Fareham, 7 September 1938			
Class	Number	Working	Notes
L12	425	Brighton – Bournemouth EP	
D15	466	Portsmouth – Bristol EP	
'700'	325	Goods	
A12	599	Gosport OP	
C2X	2548	? – Romsey OP?	
L11	441	EP from Bournemouth	
D15	471	OP to Portsmouth	
T9	721	OP to Portsmouth	
M7	480	Eastleigh – Alton OP	
T1	8	OP from Alton?	Returned later
M7	129	OP to Alton	
T9	121	Portsmouth – Southampton OP	
GW 93XX	9319	OP Reading? - Portsmouth	
S15	505	Fast freight	
L12	(425)	Bournemouth – Brighton EP	
T9	287	Portsmouth – Southampton OP	
K10	141	Alton goods	
A12	637	OP from?	
T1	11	Goods, Eastleigh – Portsmouth	
L12	424	Plymouth – Brighton EP	
I3	2085	Cardiff – Brighton EP	Unusual?
M7	242	Eastleigh – Portsmouth OP	
I3	2088	? – Portsmouth	
'700'	699	Fast freight	
L11; L12; T9; D15; '700'; T1	169, 408; 417; 115, 286, 712; 467/70; 308; 20	Unidentified workings	

I have quite a vivid memory of all those LSW 4-4-0s -- and the loud "haaaa" noise their blowers made.

On some days in January 1939 I used to go to the far end of Platform 1 at **Brighton**, where the West Coast lines curved round quite close to the Locomotive Depot, and stay for hours – but times and workings were not recorded. On **14 January**, I saw:- S15 837, L12 433, D 1730, B1 1454, B4X 2042, U1 1904, K 2339/48, '700' 690, C2X 252/52, J1 2325, I1X 2595, 2602, I3 2075/7, E3 2169, E4 2485/6, 2505/12/56/66, E5 2572/93, P 1323, E1 2122/53, 2609/90/1, A1X 2627, D1 2226/7/53, D3 2372. On **16 January**:- N15 794 'Sir Ector de Maris', S15 835/7, L12 417/31, D 1057, 1586, 1742, F1 1078, B4 2051, B4X 2045/52, K 2341, C2X 2445, 2529/46, J2 2326, I1X 2001/5, 2595/7, I3 2023/79/83, I4 2034, E4 2486, 2511/66, E5 2400, 2567/84/93, E6 2415, P 1323, 1557, E1 212/69, 2609/90/1, A1X 2689, 515S, D1 2224/9/99, 2606/25/31, D3 2383. This remarkable variety of locomotives, some of which were withdrawn even before the War, seem quite a feast compared to later on: observations at Brighton Shed on several occasions in post-war years will be listed later.

I made several journeys to and from **Brighton** (also Seaford) in 1936-40, but only those when I recorded locations as well as numbers seem worth citing here. Thus on **26 April 1939**, I travelled from **Gloucester** to **Brighton**, changing at **Reading**

EP = Express Passenger / OP = Ordinary Passenger

and Redhill; my SR observations were the following. At Reading (SR)[5] F1 1042, 1195, 1231, N 1830, U 1612/21/31/4/7, C2X 2529, H16 517/8, M7 324; at Wokingham '700' 693; at North Camp U 1637; at Guildford S11 395, T9 714, U 1616, G6 260/9/70, 348/9, M7 43, 0-4-0T 3458 'Ironside'[6]; at Redhill D 1488, 1586, F1 1043, N 1840, E4 2560/82; at Horley C2X 2437; at Three Bridges C2X 2538, E4 2514, E1 2153; at Brighton B1 1457, B4 2044, J2 2326, D1 2699. Returning on **26 July** for the Summer Holidays, I came back from **Seaford to Horsley** (with four changes) and noted the following. At Newhaven B4X 2043, C2X 2534, E4 2482/90, 2559, E4X 2489, D3 2373; at Lewes E4 2559; at Brighton D 1742, H1 2038 'Portland Bill', 2041 'Peveril Point', B4 2062, B4X 2067, N 1869, K 2344, C2X 2445, I1X 2595, I3 2080, I4 2034, E4 2498, E5 2572, E1 2153, 2609, D3 2370/91, D1 2299; at Three Bridges K 2347, C2X

2545, E4 2562, at Redhill D 1730, L1 1754, U 1617/36[7], O1 1430, C2X 2441, I3 2076, E5 2590, R1 1700, D3 2376/84/97; at Shalford C 1714; at Guildford N 1837/75, U 1612/4.

On **29 July** I went from Horsley via **Guildford** – where I noted:- U 1617, '700' 692, G6 269/70, M7 127 and D1 2229 – to **Woking** *(Table 3)*. There I enjoyed my first Summer Saturday on the SR and the record provides a glimpse of the steam passenger traffic on the main line from Waterloo at its height just before the War. It was a very exciting day for me: I was not yet 13, but I seem to have been able to read destination running-boards on the coaches as they swept by. I also had with me the current *Bradshaw* and I still have it, so I have been able to identify the trains with reasonable certainty. A day at Woking in the War, five years later, was somewhat different - see 1944 below.

Time	Class	Number	Working	Notes
TABLE 3: Woking, Saturday 29 July 1939				
10.40	S15	845	Up freight	
	'0395'	3439	Shunting	
	N	1413	Freight	
	G6	258	Goods	
	M7	43	Light engine	
	N15	748 'Vivien'	?07.30 Exeter – Waterloo	
	Lord Nelson	865 'Sir John Hawkins'	10.24 Waterloo – Ilfracombe	
	'700'	700	Down Coal train	
11.00	Lord Nelson	864 'Sir Martin Frobisher'	Down 'Bournemouth Belle', 10.30 ex-Waterloo	
	U	1632	Up Light Engine	
	N15	777 'Sir Lamiel'	10.35 Waterloo – Ilfracombe	ACE 1st Part
	V	931 'King's Wimbledon'	08.30 Bournemouth West – Waterloo	
	N15	773 'Sir Lavaine'	Down Ocean Line Express	
	H15	332	10.40 Waterloo - Padstow	ACE 2nd Part
	D15	470	08.50 Portsmouth & Southsea via Eastleigh – Waterloo	
	N15	745 'Tintagel'	10.54 Waterloo – Bude/Padstow	ACE 3rd Part
	T14	444	10.38 Waterloo - Bournemouth Central	
	U	1613	10.27 OP Waterloo – Basingstoke	
	Lord Nelson	862 'Lord Collingwood'	11.00 Waterloo – Plymouth (Friary)/Bude/Padstow	ACE 4th Part
11.30	N15	747 'Elaine'	Relief Waterloo – Ilfracombe	
	Lord Nelson	851 'Sir Francis Drake'	10.47 Waterloo Bournemouth Central	
	N15	450 'Sir Kay'	09.03 OP Templecombe – Waterloo	
	T14	443	11.22 Waterloo - Swanage	
	N15	778 'Sir Pelleas'	11.30 Waterloo – Bournemouth West	
	L12	423	11.38 Waterloo – Lymington Pier	
	V	929 'Malvern'	09.20 Swanage – Waterloo	
	N15	737 'King Uther'	10.12 Bournemouth West – Waterloo	
12.15	N15	739 'King Leodegrance'	11.45 Waterloo – Exmouth	
	M7	22	Down Light Engine	
	N15X	2333 'Remembrance'	09.25 Weymouth – Waterloo	
	S11	396	11.54 OP Waterloo Basingstoke	
	G6	260	Shunting	
	N15	736 'Excalibur'	12.00 Waterloo – Sidmouth/Exeter	
	U	1798	Down 'LMS train'	Not identified - ? Special
	N15	790 'Sir Villiars'	12.05 Waterloo – Lyme Regis/Seaton	
	D15	461	12.22 Waterloo – Swanage	
12.45	U	1618	12.12 OP Basingstoke – Waterloo	
	N15	755 'The Red Knight'	12.30 Waterloo – Bournemouth West	
	V	930 'Radley'	12.35 Waterloo – Weymouth	
	N15	774 'Sir Gaheris'	09.10 Exmouth via Budleigh Salterton/10.23 Seaton/10.28 Lyme Regis – Waterloo	
	H15	333	11.54 OP Waterloo – Salisbury	
	N15	754 'The Green Knight'	?11.10 Lymington Pier – Waterloo	
	N15	455 'Sir Launcelot'	13.00 Waterloo – Ilfracombe/Torrington	
	T14	446	13.04 Waterloo – Exeter	
	N15	451 'Sir Lamorak'	08.25 Plymouth (Friary) – Waterloo	
	D15	468	11.03 OP Portsmouth & Southsea via Eastleigh – Waterloo	
	N15	753 'Melisande'	13.22 Waterloo - Swanage	

Table 3 continued.

13.40	N15	785 'Sir Mador de la Porte'	11.08 Bournemouth West – Waterloo	
	L11	167	12.39 OP Waterloo – Basingstoke	
	H15	491	13. 30 Waterloo Bournemouth West	
	V	927 'Clifton'	11.20 Swanage – Waterloo	
	T9	282	Up Imperial Airways Express, ? from Bournemouth	Only 2 – 3 coaches!
	N15	752 'Linette'	11.25 Weymouth – Waterloo	
	D15	470	12.54 OP Waterloo – Basingstoke	
	T14	462	14.00 Waterloo – Ilfracombe/Padstow	
	U	1611	Down Light Engine	
	D15	469	Up Milk	
	N15X	2327 'Trevithick'	Down Ocean Liner Express	
	N15	738 'King Pellinore'	10.38 Exmouth via Budleigh Salterton/11.09 Sidmouth – Waterloo	
	V	925 'Cheltenham'	Relief Bournemouth West – Waterloo	
	T14	445	14.24 Waterloo - Weymouth	
	V	932 'Blundell's'	14.24 Waterloo – Swanage	
14.30	V	(931 'King's Wimbledon')	14.35 Waterloo – Weymouth	
	N15	746 'Pendragon'	11.05 Exeter – Waterloo	
	T9	730	Up OP 13.06 OP Andover Jct. – Waterloo	
	N15	742 'Camelot'	09.00 Torrington/Ilfracombe – Waterloo	
	U	1797	14.15 OP Basingstoke – Waterloo	
	U	(1617)	13.54 OP Waterloo – Basingstoke	
	Lord Nelson	(865 'Sir John Hawkins')	10.10 Ilfracombe – Waterloo	Up ACE 1st Part
	N15	(450 'Sir Kay')[8]	10.22 Torrington – Waterloo	Up ACE 2nd Part
	N15X	2332 'Stroudly'	13.05 Relief Waterloo – Exmouth/Bude	
	N15	787 'Sir Menadeuke'	10.30 Ilfracombe – Waterloo	
	H15	482	Up Empty vans and horse-boxes	
	U	1633	13.30 Lymington Pier – Waterloo	
	N15	748 'Vivien'	15.24 Waterloo – Lyme Regis/Seaton	
	H15	330	15.30 Waterloo – Southampton Terminus	Not a Boat Train
	T14	447	13.11 Bournemouth West – Waterloo	
16.00	H15	478	15.15 OP Basingstoke – Waterloo	
	H15	484	15 35 Relief Waterloo – Bournemouth	
	N15X	2329 'Stephenson'	Up Ocean Liner Express	
	D15	471	Up Fish	
	L12	434	Up empty stock (LMS)	Cf. Down train above.
	H15	(332)	10.25 Padstow – Waterloo	Up ACE 3rd Part
	N15X	2331 'Beattie'	11.35 Ilfracombe – Waterloo	Up ACE 4th Part

This page - *No. 77180, one of the numerous 'Austerity' 2-8-0s acquired from the War Department (WD) after their war service on the Continent and still retaining its Westinghouse brake-pump, draws a freight train out of Bricklayers Arms Yard at North Kent West Junction, 10 January 1948.*

Opposite bottom – *The Goods and Shed Yards outside Reading South on 5 July 1952, with SE&C Wainwright D class 4-4-0 No. 31586 nearest and further over an LSW Drummond T9 class 4-4-0 and two LB&SC Stroudley E1 class 0-6-0Ts.*

During the War, the Railways had to take on a great burden. They were still by far the most important form of land transport, other than for very short distances. They now had to operate under very difficult circumstances: the Black-Out, air raids, labour shortage and some terrible winter weather. Almost all freight and mineral traffic, including much that had previously gone by sea, had to be moved by rail and for longer distances, resulting in nearly 50% more ton-miles being conveyed. Passenger traffic rose above peacetime levels also, as war production and mobilisation of the Forces mushroomed, with people and their jobs being dispersed all over the country. As all oil (and rubber) had to be imported, motor traffic was severely curtailed. Travel for any purpose other than essentials was discouraged, almost all excursion and holiday trains disappeared and even the basic timetables were slashed – especially for long-distance trains. However, great numbers of people *had* to travel, many for long distances and without a doubt rail travel in wartime could be quite an ordeal. You often could not find a seat – and seats could not be reserved, people and their baggage, especially Servicemen with their bulky kit, jammed the corridors and on some main lines at holiday times few Relief trains were provided and people got stranded because they were physically unable to get on the trains. I, on the other hand, *enjoyed* riding on trains: if I could not secure a seat facing forward by a window on the right-hand side, in order to see trains coming the other way I preferred to sit on my suitcase in a right-hand corridor or even lean out of the window – and I never travelled by night if I could avoid it. However, my mother was working in Liverpool 1939-41, then in London, so I did a lot of travelling in the school holidays, including to various other places where my mother went for brief holidays away from the Blitz and took me with her.

In the early years of the War especially, I was not much involved or concerned with what was going on. I was only 13 when the War broke out and was away in the country both at boarding-school and in most of my holidays. On the railways, I hankered after the excitements of the holiday traffic of my first Summer Saturdays pre-war, but being primarily concerned with

engine-numbers I was certainly interested in the strange inter-company transfers of locomotives and then in the new war types – not least the 'Yanks' (the USA S160 2-8-0s). I did not really appreciate the great increase in freight and Special Government traffic until later in the War. From September 1940 until July 1944 I went to boarding-school on the Somerset & Dorset (S&DJ), which was very much a backwater in wartime. Apart from my favourite train-watching spots in London: Stratford, Old Oak Common, West Hampstead and Kenton – yes, and sometimes Clapham Junction, my principal observations were made on the LMS Birmingham – Bristol main line. For me, the main excitements came in 1944: the build-up for the Invasion of Northwest Europe (D-Day and after). When special traffic on the railways was at its zenith, in July I experienced some of the Flying Bombs in London, then left School and worked briefly at Heaton Loco in Newcastle, before going to University in London in October 1944 – so otherwise I was 'exposed' merely to the Rockets.

On **7 September** – three days after the Outbreak of World War Two and just missing the Evacuation Traffic – I travelled from **Gloucester via Reading and Guildford to Horsley**, noting:- at Reading (SR) F1 1140, R 1336; at Wokingham U 1631; at Blackwater C2X 2525; at North Camp N 1402; at Ash M7 246; at Guildford A12 643, G6 269/70.

At the end of that term at school on **19 December,** I travelled from **Seaford via London (Victoria and Paddington) to Gloucester**[9]. My SR observations were:- Newhaven: C2X 2539/57, E4 2482/94; Lewes: C2X 2443, E4 2566; Plumpton: E5 2593; Haywards Heath: E4 2557; Three Bridges: S15 834, C2X 2554, E4 2493, 2519; Redhill: F1 1195, N 1861, C 1589, E4 2507/58/60; East Croydon: H1 2041 'Peveril Point', D1 1743, E3 2170, E4 2578; Clapham Junction: O2 204, M7 40, 673; LNE N1 4559; Battersea: N15 766 'Sir Geraint', N 1813, N1 1877, W 1911, I3 2082, H 1503: Reading (SR): F1 1079, U 1628, R 1336, R1 1069.

My Christmas holidays were – to my delight – extended that year on account of the unprecedented snow and ice (freezing

Outside the Shed at Eastleigh on 11 July 1946 are two rare old engines: former Plymouth, Devonport & South-Western Junction (PDSWJ) 0-6-0T No. 756 'A.S. Harris' and LSW Drummond C14 class 0-4-0T No. 3744.

rain), which held up rail traffic over much of the country and on the SR necessitated electric trains being hauled by steam engines: I was not able to go back from Gloucester to Seaford (via London) until 2 February 1940, but I have lost any written record I made. When I went home for the Easter Holidays on **5 April 1940** I noted on the SR:- Seaford: E4 2492; Newhaven: C2X 2438, I1X 2596, E4 2566, E1 2133; Lewes: C2X 2434, I1X 2600; Haywards Heath: E4 2515, E5 2399; Three Bridges: K 2350, C 1317, E4 2577, E1 2147; Redhill: F1 1151/83, 1231, B1 1448, N 1863, U 1612, O1 1106, E4 2507/58/60/82; Coulsdon South: C2X 2549; East Croydon: E4 2479; Clapham Junction: G6 259; Victoria: N15 766 'Sir Geraint', I3 2021, H 1553; Reading (SR): U1 1797, H16 517, R 1070.

I returned to School – for my last term at that horrid prep-school – on **7 May,** by the same route except that I went down to **Seaford** from **London Bridge** and had to change at Lewes into a Seaford branch train that at that time was a *steam push-and-pull*[10]. That day I noted:- Reading (SR): F1 1043/78, 1183, U 1611/21/31/4/8, H16 519, R 1070; London Bridge: V 904 'Lancing', B4 2042; New Cross Gate: E4 2564, E6 2409/18; Norwood Junction/Yard: C2X 2535, W 1914, E4X 2477/8, 0-6-0DE 1, 3; East Croydon: I1X 2010, E5 2591; Redhill: U 1639, 1801, N1 1876; Three Bridges: I1X 2596, E1 2147; Lewes: N 1812, C2X 2543, E4 2482; Newhaven: C2X 2536/9, E4 2492/9, E1 2133; Seaford: D1 2244 (my P&P engine).

When France fell, the school summer term was terminated prematurely and as it was my Last Term I was sent home on **18 June 1940** – to my great delight, as at age 13 I was less concerned with the awful international situation unfolding than in my own private world. In retrospect I wish I had taken more detail of what I saw on the railways that day, rather than being absorbed primarily in 'collecting numbers'! Anyway, on my own I travelled from **Seaford** up to **Victoria,** then on from **Paddington** to **Gloucester**, noting down the following (SR numbers only) – not very much, it seems:- Newhaven: C2X 2438; E4 2482/92; Haywards Heath: E5 2400; Three Bridges: E1 2122/47; Purley: C3 2302; South Croydon: H1 2037 'Selsey Bill'; East Croydon: E5 2574; Windsor Bridge Junction: 0-6-0DE 3; Victoria: E2 2107; Reading (SR): F1 1183; H16 517; R1 1070.

(My most notable observation that day was actually of LNER Pacific 4481 'St Simon' at Southall).

For the rest of the year I was well away from the SR, although in September 1940 I began four long years at Bryanston School near Blandford. This was on the celebrated S&D, which was at any rate 'half-Southern'. The track and signalling on the S&D was maintained by the SR. The motive power, however, was normally very LMS, but during the War the LMSR borrowed a number of SR locomotives and these were put to work on the S&D particularly. A number of other SR locomotives were put to work on the LMSR – and LNER and GWR - elsewhere. The SR locomotives put to work on the S&D comprised the whole of the ex-LSW Class S11 4-4-0s, also six Class T1 0-4-4Ts, along with two T9s for short periods, so the S11s became very familiar to me in my schooldays. The S&D had an exiguous passenger service during the war – with only one train that could be considered an express (09.45 from Bournemouth West to Derby); freight traffic was not heavy and owing to the line being single over long stretches and with heavy gradients it did not convey much special wartime traffic and was a distinct backwater in the War. We could barely see the line from Bryanston School – only hear the occasional freight at night struggling up the 1-in-80 northward out of Blandford, but I was never tempted to go and 'watch trains' at Blandford – only to go on the occasional illicit expedition further afield as a senior boy.

On **20 September 1940** I noted just 18 engines on all the 53 miles after **Bath (Queen Square)** all the way to **Blandford**; only three of these were SR, all at Templecombe where S&D trains crept up into the SR station and stopped for ages:- N15 456 'Sir Galahad', 751 'Etarre'; U 1795. Then for the three months of the Autumn Term I saw trains only in the distance, until **20 December 1940** I travelled home (to Cheltenham) in the '10.20' from Blandford – the aforementioned Express. This train was supposed to run through Templecombe (Lower) non-stop, but it may well have been held up there, for we reached Bath an hour late and in fact I noted six SR locomotives at **Templecombe**:- N15 744 'Maid of Astolat', 779 'Sir Colgreavnce', 789 'Sir Guy'; S15 823; N 1406; U 1795. I returned to school at Blandford, from Ashchurch via

Resting outside Feltham Shed, LSW Adams '0395' class 0-6-0 No. 3167, 27 September 1947.

Mangotsfield and Bath, on **18 January 1941**. This time I noted just one SR engine, S15 825 at **Templecombe**.

At half-term, my father came down and took me out. On **22 February 1941**, he must have indulged me with a spell at **Templecombe**, for my notebook records nine SR numbers:- N15 454 'Queen Guinevere', 766 'Sir Geraint', 772 'Sir Percivale', 792 'Sir Hervis de Revel', S15 829/32, U 1790, T9 122, '700' 317; also five LMS. Then on **Sunday 23 February** he escorted me on my first ever Shed Visit, to **Bournemouth Shed!** There I noted 37 engines:- 'Lord Nelson' 856 'Lord St Vincent', 859 'Lord Hood'; N15 736 'Excalibur', 737 'King Uther', 742 'Camelot', 751 'Etarre'; H15 478; S15 506, 843; V 924 'Haileybury', 925 'Cheltenham', 926 'Repton', 930 'Radley', 931 'King's Wimbledon'; D15 473; K10 394; L11 165/73, 438; L12 424/9/30; T9 113, 338, 728; X6 658; Q 540; '700' 690; M7 21/8, 50, 104/6/7, 245/55; B4 100. At the end of term on **29 March 1941**, I travelled home again on the '10.20', but saw no SR engines at all. On my return to Blandford on **2 May** I saw just one: L11 163 at **Templecombe**.

At half-term my father came again and this time (**23 June 1941**)[11] accompanied me watching trains at **Salisbury** for about 1½ hours; also, thanks to his persuasive powers, we also visited the Loco Depot. My notes show just numbers and no workings or even which engines I noted on Shed, but the occasion is memorable to me as on Shed was the pioneer *Bulleid Pacific*, 21C1 'Channel Packet'. This strange new beast had first come out of Eastleigh Works on **17 February**, and after various trials had only started regular work from Salisbury on **4 June** – the enginemen seemed excited about it. Including at the Shed, that day at Salisbury I noted 76 locomotives, comprising five GWR and the following SR:- 'Merchant Navy' 21C1 'Channel Packet', 'Lord Nelson' 850 'Lord Nelson', 859 'Lord St Vincent', 862 'Lord Collingwood', 864 'Sir Martin Frobisher'; N15 449 'Sir Torre', 450 'Sir Kay', 451 'Sir Lamorak', 452 'Sir Meliagrance', 453 'King Arthur', 454 'Queen Guinevere', 456 'Sir Galahad', 737 'King Uther'; 739 'King Leodegrance', 747 'Elaine', 773 'Sir Lavaine', 776 'Sir Galagars', 778 'Sir Pelleas', 787 'Sir Menadeuke', 788 'Sir Urre of the Mount', 789 'Sir Guy', 790 'Sir Villiars; H15 332/4, 476/7; S15 502/5, 829/31;

S11 395; L11 405; L12 432; T9 117, 714/5/8/27; D15 463/71; B4 2044/51/68/74; B4X 2043/71; N 1850; U 1612/3/8/24/36, 1794/5; '700' 315/7, 691; '0395' 3441; A12 646/54; I3 2084/7/8/9; G6 237/79; T1 10; M7 41, 60, 243, 675.

The journey at the end of the Summer Term, again by the S&D to Bath, produced no SR engines. I watched trains at many interesting places during the summer holidays, including Oxford where I used to see the curious wartime Ashford – Newcastle express[12], which was worked to Banbury by a U1. Only on **4 September,** when I travelled up to Paddington from Oxford for the day, did I see any other SR, at Reading (SR): F1 1105, N 1839/69, U 1614/27/35, U1 1897, '700' 308, 695. However, by the time I went back to school from Cheltenham on **19 September** the SR loans to the LMS were at work on the S&D and I saw, to my great surprise:- S11 398, 402 and T9 305 at **Bath** and S11 403 at **Sturminster Newton**; also, on the SR at **Templecombe**, T9 314, 714 and U 1793. On my journey home on **19 December**, S11 401 piloted my train's LMS 2P 4-4-0 696 from Evercreech Junction to Bath and I also noted S11 396 at Blandford and T1 6 (also loaned) at Templecombe.

That winter, my mother began to live in London. From then on I saw much more of the SR in my school holidays and thereafter. On **29 December 1941**, I took a trip down to Tilbury, over on the ferry and back to **Charing Cross from Gravesend (Central),** noting:- R 1666 (on the Port Victoria Branch train) and C 1692 at Gravesend; C 1270 at Dartford; O1 1389 at Plumstead; O1 1397 at Woolwich Arsenal; D 1746 at Rotherhithe Road; I1 1546 at London Bridge; V 938 'St Olave's', L 1777 and L1 1788 at Charing Cross. No doubt, it being winter and with netting over the carriage windows I missed several other engine-numbers. Then on **2 January 1942** I nosed around the Battersea area amongst all the bombed streets, and noted the following. At **Nine Elms:-** 754 'The Green Knight', 779 'Sir Colgrevance', 781 'Sir Aglovale'; H15 482/90/1; S15 507; T14 446; L11 156; D15 464; G6 259, 353; 0-6-0T 756 'A.S. Harris'; M7 38, 667: at **Stewarts Lane/Queens Road:-** N15 452 'Sir Meliagrance', 802 'Sir Durnore'; L11 442; D1 1246; C 1682/94; I3 2090; E4 2479; E2 2106/8; M7 40; H 1005, 1263/5; also LNER J52 3963 and GW 57XX 3642. On **3 January**, I travelled from **Barnes to**

13

Waterloo, noting:- H 1329 at Barnes; '700' 701 at Wandsworth Town; N15 775 'Sir Agravaine', M7 33, 123, also LMS 0-6-0 3261 at Clapham Junction; T14 448, V 927 'Clifton', N 1811, G6 160 at Nine Elms; 'Lord Nelson' 855 'Robert Blake', N15 450 'Sir Kay', 456 'Sir Galahad', N15X 2333 'Remembrance', U 1616 at Waterloo. On **7 January**, I nosed round **London Bridge** and **Battersea** again, noting:- V 903 'Charterhouse', L 1776, B4X 2067, I3 2021, also LMS 2-6-2T 35 at London Bridge; and at Stewarts Lane/Queens Road N15 767 'Sir Valence', 794 'Sir Ector de Maris', E1 1497, U 1617, U1 1902/9, C 1499, C2X 2451, I3 2082, W 1922, E2 2100, M7 123, H 1311/20/9, D1 2215, also GW 57XX 8764.

On **22 January,** I went back to Bryanston School, from Ashchurch via Mangotsfield and Bath, this time seeing one of Bath Shed's loaned SR engines (S11 401) at **Gloucester,** as well as on the S&D:- S11 399 at Bath (Queen Square), whence S11 404 was my train engine to Blandford and I saw T9 304 at Stalbridge and T1 4 at Sturminster Newton. At half-term, on **28 February**, I went from **Blandford** to **Bournemouth West** and back, S11 403 being the train-engine on the return journey. I noted:- X2 586 and M7 106 at Poole; T9 304, 719, M7 254 at Branksome; N15 779 'Sir Colgrevance', L12 415, M7 47 at Bournemouth West in the morning. In the evening, N15 777 'Sir Lamiel', V 926 'Repton', M7 50; M7 104 at Branksome; M7 22 at Poole; S11 400 at Bailey Gate. The S11s were now working all the time on the S&D, but on the journey home on **1 April** , via Bath to Cheltenham, the only SR engine I noted was S11 404 at Blandford.

In London in the holidays and subsequently, my favourite train-watching spots were not on the SR, but I occasionally had a session at **Clapham Junction**, which would have been truly incomparable as a 'Resort for Rail Fans' twenty and more years earlier, before the wholesale electrification of the intensive suburban and many of the long-distance passenger services. However, there was still a variety of Steam to be seen there: on the expresses out of Waterloo and the Oxted line trains out of Victoria. As well there was varied and interesting freight traffic that brought as well as SR steam engines many GW, LMS and LNER. There were massive amounts of freight constantly moving through and round London, over the 'inner-ring' lines that interconnected the main lines, not least over the WLR/ WLER[13] through Clapham Junction. However, banned to SR engines were the most important London links of all: those over Blackfriars Bridge, by Snow Hill Tunnel and the MWL* to and from the LNER (GN Section) and the LMS (Midland Section), also the East London Line from New Cross/(Gate) under the Thames to the LNE (GE Section), although both routes were also restricted to short trains hauled by small tank locomotives. Anyway, 'foreign' workings were very evident at Clapham Junction. Moreover, during the War, movement of freight was not suspended during the rush-hours, as it was in peacetime.

SR engines worked between their major Yards at Feltham, Nine Elms, Battersea, Norwood Junction, Hither Green, Herne Hill and Bricklayers Arms, also to the GWR Yards at Old Oak Common[14], the LMS at Willesden and Brent and right round to the LNER Yards at Neasden and Temple Mills, all these trips being worked reciprocally with the 'foreign' engines[15]. SR locomotives worked freight off the N&SWJ to and from **Brent**

Sidings (Cricklewood): thus on **10 April 1942,** amongst all the LMS locomotives I recorded in a couple of hours, I noted H15 477/90 and '700' 327.

On **13 April** I went from **Waterloo to Feltham**, observed there for an hour or two, then returned to **Waterloo**, noting:- V 931 'King's Wimbledon', M7 322 at Waterloo; H15 333 at Vauxhall; N15 751 'Etarre', H2 'The Needles', G6 271, 354 at Nine Elms; K10 391, N 1414, U1 1900, C2x 2451, M7 38, 241 and LMS 0-4-4T 1379 at Clapham Junction; H 1544 at Wandsworth Town; K10 385 at Twickenham. At Feltham in the Yard or at the Shed I noted:- N15 753 'Melisande', S15 843, L11 167, 440, D1 1247, 1492, '700' 352/68, 694/5/7, '0395' 3163, G16 492/3/4 (the Hump shunters), H16 517/8, M7 32 and LNE J52 4235. On the return journey I noted:- K10 341 at Putney; L11 155, T9 119, M7 667 and LMS 0-6-0 4348 at Clapham Junction; H 1320 at Pouparts Junction; G6 259 at Nine Elms; V 926 'Repton' at Waterloo. On the same day, I did another round trip crossing the Thames on a ferry, this time the Woolwich Ferry. On the return by SR from Woolwich Arsenal to Waterloo (East), I noted:- C 1723 at Charlton; C 1090 at Blackheath; H 1551 at Rotherhithe Road; N15 803 'Sir Harry le Fise Lake', V 901 'Winchester', E 1157, I3 2086 at London Bridge; V 903 'Charterhouse', 907 'Dulwich' at Waterloo (East). Then, on **14 April** I had another stint at **Queens Road/Stewarts Lane** and noted:- 'Lord Nelson' 861 'Lord Anson', 863 'Lord Rodney', 864 'Sir Martin Frobisher'; N15 452 'Sir Meliagrance', 784 'Sir Nerovens', 802 'Sir Durnore'; H15 478/90; V 916 'Whitgift', 932 'Blundell's', K10 380; L12 427; L 1761; B4X 2060; N1 1822; U1 1903/4; C 1576; W 1912/5; I1X 2007; I3 2028; M7 322; H 1263/4/5, 1503/53; LNE J52 3974 and GW 57XX 8750. On **16 April** I went down from **Charing Cross** to **New Cross Gate** and back, and noted:- N15 767 'Sir Valence'; V 909 'St Paul's', 914 'Eastbourne', 934 'St Lawrence', 939 'Leatherhead'; L 1772 at Charing Cross/Cannon Street; E6 2411/8 at New Cross Gate; around Bricklayers Arms Junction: V 907 'Dulwich'; E 1516; N 1863; K 2344; O1 1380/1; I1X 2006; I3 2023; E3 2460; LMS 0-6-0T 7218 and LNE N1 4565/90/5.

When I returned to school, again from Cheltenham via Bath, on **1 May 1942,** I noted SR engines working on the S&D:- T1 1[16] at Evercreech Junction and at Templecombe S11 397 and T1 6, as well as K10 344 and U 1793 on the SR. At the Summer Half-Term, I went from **Blandford** to **Bournemouth West** and back on **20 June**, noting – apart from just three LMS:- S11 404 at Blandford; M7 107, 318 at Broadstone; V 928 'Stowe' at Bournemouth West; M7 50 at Branksome; T1 363 at Parkstone; M7 22 at Poole; S11 399 at Bailey Gate. On **21 June** I went to **Salisbury** by bus and noted:- N15 452 'Sir Meliagrance', 788 'Sir Urre of the Mount'; H15 331, 475; S15 508, 823/32; T9 314; U 1796; '700' 350; T1 361; M7 60. Again the next day (**22 June**) I went to **Salisbury**, took a train to **Basingstoke**, spent an hour or two there on the platform and returned to Salisbury; the train engine on the outward journey was B4X 2073[17], on the return it was U 1622. I noted:- N15 746 'Pendragon'; S15 828; Q 538; B4X 2073; Z 957; I3 2087; T1 361 at Salisbury; 'Lord Nelson' 856 'Lord St Vincent'; A12 649 at Grateley; U 1636, also GW 43XX 5345 and 45XX 4521, at Andover Junction; T14 444 at Whitchurch; H2 2423 'The Needles' at Worting Junction. Then at **Basingstoke** (*Table 4*) – probably c. 13.00 – 15.00:-

MWL = Metropolitan Widened Lines.

Class	Number	Working	Notes
	TABLE 4: Basingstoke, 22 June 1942		
H2; D1; U	2422 'North Foreland', 2424 'Beachy Head'; 1145; 1632	On Shed?	
T9	726	Station pilot	
T9	714	Iron-ore empties	*Where on earth from?!*
'Lord Nelson'	853 'Sir Richrad Grenville'	? 12.10 Bournemouth West - Waterloo	
N15	738 'King Pellinore'	Down Troop train	
Q1	C1	Down freight	New 0-6-0 Class!
N	1851	Up 'coal'	
U	1629	Up Slow	
N15	782 'Sir Brian'	Light engine	
H15	330	Down OP	
'Lord Nelson'	854 'Howard of Effingham'	Up EP	
L12	416	Light engine	
'Lord Nelson'	850 'Lord Nelson'	Up EP, stopping	
N15	454 'Queen Guinevere'	Down EP, stopping	
L12	423	?	
V	929 'Malvern'	Down EP	
S15	506	Down 'coal'	
'Lord Nelson'	859 'Lord Hood'	Up EP	
V	926 'Repton'	Down EP	
H2	2421 'North Foreland'	Down Local Goods	
U	1622	Light engine and OP later to Salisbury	
G6	265	Shunting	
GW 'Hall'	4994 'Downton Hall'	OP from Reading	
V	930 'Radley'	Down Bournemouth EP	
H15; U; Q	488; 1630; 548	In Yard/Shed	

On the return journey I noted:- L11 407 at Overton; N15 451 'Sir Lamorak'; X6 664 at Andover Junction; M7 60 at Porton (Amesbury branch); 'Lord Nelson' 860 'Lord Hawke'; H15 334; U 1795; M7 675 and GW 'Bulldog' 3438 at Salisbury.

On the journey home on **29 July 1942** from Blandford via Bath to Cheltenham, the SR engines I noted on the S&D were only T1 6 at Templecombe and S11 399 at Bath, but I also saw K10 137 (on loan to Gloucester LMS) at **Stonehouse**. During those summer holidays I watched trains at **Ashchurch** quite often: on **1 August**, S11 403 (of Bath) came through on an Up empties. Later I travelled up to the Peak District to accompany my mother on her week's holiday and we stayed at a hotel at Ambergate that turned out to be ideal for me as it was right next to the Station! On **31 August**, after travelling up from St Pancras to Derby with my mother, I got her to accompany me by bus to Long Eaton in order to explore Toton Yard and to my joy I found it was possible to walk all along next to it on the east side – and I was exhilarated, and projected my enthusiam to my mother. Of course the immense railway traffic and countless engines were almost all *LMS*, but at Derby I noted loaned SR F1 No. 1060 and B1 1441 (with red-hot smokebox from its exertions) and at Toton I noted F1 1156. The next day, **1 September**, I saw A12 No. 618 at **Derby**, which was one of five A12s loaned to the WD and was working on the Melbourne Military Railway. On returning to St Pancras from Nottingham on 5 September, in spite of it being Saturday I noted a veritable feast – 233 – of engine-numbers, all LMS but one -- new SR Q1 C8 at Brent Sidings. On **7 September** I went from **London Bridge** to **Hither Green** and back from Grove Park, to try to see the Shed and Yards. I failed to see much, but what I noted were:- V 915 'Brighton', 935 'Sevenoaks'; I1X 2003; LNE N1 4559 at London Bridge; H 1540 at Rotherhithe Road; C 1584 at Lewisham; F1 1110, 1249, O1 1123, 1374, C 1061, 1227, 1576, Z 953, LNE N1 4552 at Hither Green; E 1491 at Grove Park; V 906 'Sherborne' at New Cross; H 1533 at London Bridge.

In those days, I was also very interested in collecting railway *tickets* dropped outside stations – which if not too dirty proved of considerable value in recent years! On **8 September** I *bought* one to Blackfriars at Holborn Viaduct[18](!): then after going by Tube to South Wimbledon and walking to Merton Park to look for tickets, I came back from Wimbledon (where I saw H15 483) to **Clapham Junction** and spent about 90 minutes there *(Table 5)*, before returning to Victoria – where I saw V 913 'Christ's Hospital' and L 1762. The sample of steam locomotive observations I made in a 90 minute morning session in 1942 can be compared with my sessions there after the War, to be presented later.

LSW Drummond T14 class 'Paddlebox' 4-6-0 passing Vauxhall on the milk empties for the West Country (Chard Junction etc.), 24 April 1948.

WATCHING TRAINS on the SR – PART I

FOOTNOTES

[1] Their sisters, who on the whole don't like their brothers and anyway are more mature, have their own (feminine) interests; Train Spotting is not one of them.

[2] I also wish I'd taken more photographs of the delightful girl-friends I had – back in those Good Old Days when women were feminine and wore elegant *women's* clothes, didn't deliberately straighten their hair and had decent figures!!

[3] Until near the end of the War, in March 1945, I was 'shopped' by a suspicious fellow-passenger who handed me over to the Military Police at York. The MP, however, was nice: he didn't put me in chains or even confiscate my notebook, but merely told me not to write down anything except engine-numbers – and I only did that for the rest of *that* day anyway.

[4] We travelled from Cheltenham (Lansdown) to Southampton via Andover Junction (*i.e.* over the M&SWJ) and Romsey, then to Fareham and the Gosport branch.

[5] Before and during the War, the old SE&C F1 and B1 4-4-0s continued to work many of the passenger services between Reading and Redhill.

[6] This was a Hawthorn-Leslie 0-4-0T built for Southampton Docks, but by 1939 employed as Shed-shunter at Guildford.

[7] U 1636 took over a 'Morris Oxford Tour' train, which was brought up from Brighton by H1 2041.

[8] Multiple observations of the same locomotive are in brackets.

[9] On my own – as I recollect, as in wartime the SR did not provide the Special School Trains they had in peacetime.

[10] One of these was shot up and badly damaged by the Luftwaffe on 3 July 1940 near Bishopstone.

[11] This was the day after Hitler invaded Soviet Russia and I remember my father saying: "Now we shan't lose the War".

[12] This was primarily a Forces Leave train, but it was available to everybody (but 'Limited Accommodation') and shown in the public timetables: Ashford 08.45, Paddock Wood 09.12, Tonbridge 09.22-24, Redhill 09.54-10.00, Deepdene 10.15, Guildford 10.42-44, North Camp 11.03, Reading (GW) 11.37-40, Didcot 12.08, Oxford 12.30-35, Heyford 12.58, Banbury 13.13-27, Woodford & Hinton 13.40-48, Rugby (Central) 14.10-13, Leicester (Central) 14.42-52, Loughborough (Central) 15.06-09, Arkwright Street 15.30, Nottingham (Victoria) 15.33-36, Sheffield (Victoria) 16.43-55, Rotherham & Masboro' 17.12, Pontefract (Baghill) 17.55, York 18.25-39, Northallerton 19.15-17, Darlington 19.37-41, Durham 20.15-21, Newcastle 20.45. The Up train left Newcastle at 08.12, made the same stops (additionally at Thirsk and at Sherburn-in-Elmet, but not Heyford or Didcot) and got to Ashford at 20.32 – a 12-hour journey if anyone ever did the whole, likely to be somewhat more in practice.

[13] Abbreviations:- ACE – Atlantic Coast Express; AFV – Armoured Fighting Vehicles; DN&S – Didcot, Newbury & Southampton; EP – Express passenger; K&ESR – Kent & East Sussex Railway; Lord Nelson; M&SWJ – Midland & South-Western Junction; MWL – Metropolitan Widened Lines; N&SWJ – NLR - North London Lines, North & South Western Junction; OP – Ordinary passenger; RCTS – Railway Correspondence & Travel Society; S&D – Somerset & Dorset; WL – Windsor Lines; WLR – West London Line; WLER – West London Extension Line.

[14] Loading-gauge restrictions limited where GW locomotives could go, but their small engines could work to the Depots at South Lambeth by the WLER, also to Smithfield via the Metropolitan line.

[15] LMS engines even worked down to Three Bridges.

[16] A desirable 'Cop.!

[17] As well as loaning its surplus locomotives to the other Railways during the War, there was quite a bit of shuffling round on the SR. As on the other Railways, the larger passenger locomotives were often used for the increased freight traffic, so smaller, older engines were given more work than in peacetime. Engines off the Eastern and Central Sections – not needed for holiday traffic – were brought over to the Western Section, where also in the earlier years of the War some of the elderly Adams 4-4-0s and 0-4-2s were reinstated and put back to work. The Maunsell 2-6-0s were worked intensely on Special passenger and on freight, also 'Arthurs' and even 'Nelsons' were employed on freight working.

[18] The booking-clerk thought I was crazy!

PART 1B: WILL APPEAR IN 'WARTIME SOUTHERN PART 3'.
PART 2: THE YEARS 1945 - 1948 WILL FOLLOW SHORTLY

Left - LSW Adams T1 class 0-4-4T No. 1, alongside the back of the Up platform at Winchester, 25 October 1947.

Opposite bottom – Resplendent after overhaul at Eastleigh Works, LSW Adams G6 class 0-6-0T No. 275, 25 October 1947.

Above - B1 No. 1021 on Tonbridge 18 May 1946.

'SOUTHERN (A BIT MORE) EXPOSED'

Peter Squibb

Part 1 appeared in Issue No. 7

As my twentieth birthday approached I was made aware that my 'learning' time was coming to an end and that I should start looking for an adult position somewhere, so I began studying the vacancy sheets. An Assistant Telegraph Lineman was required at Poole and as it was fairly close to home, I applied for the post and was successful. It was not one of my better decisions, as the man I was to work with was not one of nature's communicators and seemed to resent my presence from the first day. However, I had to make the best of it, and looking back, I suppose it contributed to both my railway education and did its best to broaden my horizons.

As far as I recall the double track main lines were all signalled by Preece's 3-wire instruments, with which I was already familiar, but I was soon to discover that the Southern had some surprises for me, a characteristic that it diligently maintained until the day I finally retired in 2003: at which time I was introduced to the Irish Railways and discovered there that so far as surprises were concerned, the Southern Region was in a much lower league!

Besides the main line through Bournemouth, the 'Old Road', the original Southampton & Dorchester line, was still open although the section from Broadstone to Hamworthy Junction had been singled and was worked by token instruments. There was double track between Broadstone and Poole and the majority of up trains through Poole had come that way. The Somerset & Dorset Railway from Bath and the Midlands joined the route at Broadstone, a branch from Salisbury joined at West Moors and there was a shuttle service from Brockenhurst to Bournemouth West via Ringwood. It is difficult to reconcile all that with the situation that exists today; Bournemouth West gone and no trace of the Broadstone route visible from Holes Bay Junction at Poole. The ease with which the road lobby was enabled to deprive growing towns like Ringwood, Wimborne, Blandford, Fordingbridge, Swanage and many hundreds of others of their rail connection was highly questionable.

The Swanage Branch was worked by two different types of Tyer's Tablet instruments. From the terminus to Corfe Castle a 'No 6' was installed. These, I was given to understand, were still in fairly common use but the machines between Corfe and Worgret Junction on the main line were No 7s, a different thing altogether. Unlike the 'Bakelite' tablets in the No 6 instruments the No. 7s had metal tablets, made, I seem to recall of layers of brass and steel. This meant that they were heavy enough to drop through a slot and unlock the door of Furzebrook Siding Ground Frame, which was situated between the two signal boxes and this requirement kept the No7s in place for many years. It also contributed to a 'near miss' at Worgret Junction.

There was a pair of enginemen at Swanage who were famous for getting the maximum out of an M7 class tank. They usually came up to and around the curve at Worgret at a much higher speed than was permitted, bearing in mind they were required to drop the tablet into the hand of the signalman, but on this occasion they excelled themselves. On the day in question, the signalman was taken totally by surprise by their early arrival and was still descending the box steps when the fireman put the tablet pouch on the horn-shaped catcher. The force was such that the stitching of the leather pouch split and the tablet flew past the signalman's head at great speed. He picked up the tablet beside the up main line and swore that it was some time before his heartbeat was back to normal.

It was that same crew that saw me walking beside the line on my way back to Wareham one day and slowed to pick me up. By the time I realised what was going on the engine had passed me, so I climbed up the steps to the luggage van. As soon as they saw I was aboard they opened up and it was then that I discovered that the van door was locked. This naturally caused them some amusement; consequently I rode on the outside of the train as far as Wareham's home signal where they slowed for me to get off. Neither of us thought it a good idea to run into the station like that.

I still have no idea how tablet instruments work. Whether this is down to my mate's inadequacy as a teacher or my ineptitude as a pupil I know not, although I did learn enough to be able to carry out a tablet transfer which was necessary when

Opposite top - The yard at Weymouth, so familiar to Peter Squibb and yet now reduced to running lines and little else. Dorchester based 'U' class No. 31632 has the Bournemouth - Weymouth head code displayed just north of the station in the early 1950s. Courtesy Paul Hersey

Opposite bottom - Bill Squibb, Peter's father had started life on the GWR and was a signalman in the area for many years. He is seen in 1965 in the BR 1957 Weymouth box, which had replaced the former GWR Weymouth Station and Weymouth Junction boxes both of which closed the day the new facility was brought into operation. With a Westinghouse A3 frame of 116 this was considerably more than the 44 levers and 45 levers respectively, in the older boxes. As was then standard practice, the frame faced the rear, so giving an uninterrupted view of passing trains, at the front the windows were also angled down to reduce glare. This box closed just 30 years later in September 1987. Weymouth was destined to be the last major mechanical signalling installation on the Southern Region.

The original 1885 signal box at Corfe Castle and which lasted until 17 June 1956. After this date a second-hand 12 lever frame was installed in the station office at the north end of the building. The original design, possibly unique on the LSWR in so far as the front windows were replaced by timber, is currently being resurrected by the Swanage Railway. 6 September 1955.   *J H Aston*

tablets accumulated at one end due to an imbalance of traffic. On a branch that was a terminus, it would appear logical that if a certain number of trains head in one direction, then the same number will invariably come back; after all, they could not get lost. But in the case of the Swanage branch there was occasional double-heading to consider, the extra engine sometimes returning light or when the train was split at Swanage, hence the imbalance. (I was already familiar with the practice as we used to do it regularly between Maiden Newton to Bridport).

I was armed with the evidence that I had carried out such a transfer when I was summoned to the Salisbury office to explain myself to the bosses who claimed to have seen me the previous Wednesday at Yeovil Pen Mill, i.e. well away from my duties. The Chief Lineman at Poole had explained the charge to me, although he had been warned not to, so I knew I had to choose my words carefully. On the journey, which was via Wimborne and Fordingbridge, (in these more enlightened days it would be via Southampton) I rehearsed my defence.

I arrived at the office to find that the sub inspector, Joe Lawman, an appropriate name in the circumstances, was to be the prosecuting counsel. Inspector Lucas, the other so-called prosecution witness, took no part in the proceedings, so I suspect that he had doubts or had been asleep in the train when it stopped at Pen Mill.

"Why" said Mr Lawman "were you at Yeovil last week?"

"I wasn't" I replied.

"But we both saw you."

"You couldn't have because I wasn't there" I said. "Which day was this?" I asked, preparing to produce the names of signalmen at Swanage, Corfe and Worgret who would support my account.

"I can tell you where I was working each day last week, so when was it?

Now the proceedings descended into farce. "I can't remember" he said.

Still there was no word from Mr Lucas. Their movements for the previous week could easily have been determined but they seemed reluctant to do so.

"Well, if you say you weren't there we will have to accept it, but we both saw you."

I was sent on my way. I don't know who they saw but he was obviously a good looking young fellow who had no idea of the trouble that he almost stirred up for me! I worked under that pair for some years and relationships were always strained.

A lot of staff movement was going on at that time, due to retirement, promotion and so on, so when a vacancy occurred at Weymouth I moved, with the advantage that I could also live at home instead of in lodgings. After about six months a temporary position for the Chief Lineman at Poole meant that the Lineman at Weymouth, Stan Button, covered the job. On the first Monday morning of this arrangement, Stan was in our mess room as we completed some paperwork that he would take to Poole when a signalman called to say that a lineman at Dorchester Junction needed to speak to us. We were understandably surprised as the full complement of staff was sitting in our room.

It transpired that the Salisbury office, having no confidence in the Assistants at Weymouth, had arranged for the lineman at Poole to cover Stan's absence and had not bothered to advise us. The person concerned was highly thought of by the management, which puzzled those of us who had worked with him, as his incompetence bordered on the dangerous, a fact demonstrated some years later when a wrongly-wired ground frame produced resulted in a near miss, the possible collision only averted by a very diligent engine driver.

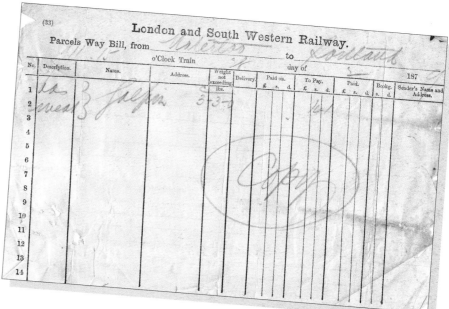

An example of some early LSWR paperwork found during a trip to Portland.

I took exception to the arrangement for two reasons. I felt that my competence was being doubted and, more importantly, Daphne and I were getting married and the higher grade of pay would be extremely useful. I wrote to the Inspector in very strong terms, so strong that the Chief Lineman asked if I really wanted it to go through. I said I did and waited. I was quite convinced that the business of being seen at Yeovil when I was nowhere near the place was still uppermost in their minds. Possibly, after discussion with Stan Button they agreed to let me do the job for a trial period, which in the end became open-ended.

The tactics of the office were demonstrated one Sunday when we were booked to replace the A.T.C. test ramps at the exit from the Weymouth engine shed. Here I must explain for the Southern devotees that Great Western engines were equipped with Automatic Train Control which advised the drivers of the aspect of a Distant signal as they approached and which, if not acknowledged when the signal was on , would bring the train to a stand. Historically, Weymouth was a Great Western shed and still had some G.W. engines although the Southern Region were in control, a situation which engendered some good-natured banter between the two factions. On occasions too, it was not so good-natured.

The test ramps, one alive, one dead, were much shorter than the real thing and replacing them was a cushy number. We had been advised by the Chief Lineman that the Inspectors would be fully involved that Sunday so how did we feel about making an early start and getting the job finished with the advantage we could have most of the day off? He obviously had something planned and we readily agreed.

The job went well and we were tightening the last screws when the Chief swore viciously.
"Take some of those screws out quickly….."

We did so, the reason being the Chief had seen the two Inspectors walking up the track from the station. Fortunately they were Southern men so had little idea of the working of A.T. C. and after some flannel and a cup of tea they left us to complete the job, again!

Then came the 'Work Study' brigade. An army of mathematicians with stop-watches and measuring wheels descended on us and seemed to take over the S&T Department. The upshot of their deliberations, as far as our depot was concerned, was that we were over-staffed and as I was the last one to be appointed I was the one who had to go. Craftily, they did not use the word 'redundant', I was instead deemed 'unallocated'. As I was still covering the lineman's position I felt fairly secure, but with marriage in the offing I naturally began to study the vacancy sheets once again.

A technician was required at Andover Junction and although having no knowledge of the place and only a vague idea where it actually was I applied for the job. Weeks went by. Daphne and I needed to find somewhere to live but where that was to be was not certain.

I made a nuisance of myself by letter and telephone and could get nowhere until one day I asked the question yet again of my old friend, Sub-Inspector Joe Lawman. His reply was typical. "I can't tell you"; he paused; "But the news is good".

For whom, I thought. In fact, it was only a day or so later that the official notification arrived and we could begin house-hunting in the Andover area. It was a move that meant we would form new friendships which have survived and in 2009 we attended two ruby wedding celebrations of friends whose weddings we had attended in Andover. Experiences on the Andover S&T district will follow in a later issue.

The name of Peter Squibb will be well known to many in the modelling fraternity. His exquisite model signals, finials with holes in the ball and working mechanical route indicators (cash-register type), are the mark of a skilled craftsman. Behind the modeller however, is a career first on the railway and later in industry. A quick-witted character, in his presence you just know he will come out with an eminently suitable quip just at the right moment. It is a privilege to record his railway life and also to count upon Peter as a personal friend for many years.

Left - Skew arch bridge No. 15 towards Corfe from Norden station. (The locomotive is No. 34028 'Eddystone'.)

Bottom *- M7 as SR No. 53 passing under skew arch bridge No. 15*

Opposite page *- Richard E Pinney, mines manager from about 1880 to 1910.*

Interested parties should contact:

Website : www.pmmmg.org

Purbeck Mineral and Mining Museum Group
Swanage Railway Trust
Station House
Swanage
Dorset. BH19 1HB.

THE MIDDLEBERE PLATEWAY: PART 2

Its History and Connections with the Early Railways of Southern England

Peter Hollins

Continued from Issue 10: April 2010

The Arrival of the LSWR.

On 17 May 1844 a meeting was held in Wareham calling together all the interested parties of Wareham and the Isle of Purbeck, with regard to the construction of the Southampton to Dorchester Railway. The meeting was chaired by William Mortimer, the mayor of Wareham. Thomas Phippard had requested the meeting and spoke of his experiences attending a meeting of the Southampton and Dorchester Railway in Southampton, chaired by Mr. Castleman, along with Mr. Chaplin from the board of the LSWR.

To Phippard's dismay he appeared to be the only representative of Purbeck at the meeting, there being strong representations from Weymouth, Dorchester and Poole. Three routes were proposed by Mr. Castleman, none of which passed near Wareham or Purbeck, the favoured route being one through Ringwood, Wimborne, thence via Bloxworth, Bere, Tinkleton and Stinsford to Dorchester. There had been correspondence between Phippard and Castleman in the intervening time and now the purpose of the meeting was to write an official petition to the Southampton & Dorchester board to fix a route prior to surveying the line. The meeting was adjourned until the following Tuesday.

Four days later, on 21 May 1844, the meeting was reconvened in Wareham calling together all the interested parties of Wareham and the Isle of Purbeck, with the addition of those who did not attend the first meeting. Amongst those present was William Pike (Pike Bros. of Furzebrook), John Hales Calcraft (MP. and land owner, B. Fayle & Co.), Freeland Filliter (solicitor) and Thomas Phippard (solicitor), who between them persuaded the gathering of the importance of a rail connection to London through the Southampton and Dorchester.

They favoured the LSWR-backed proposal of the Southampton & Dorchester, but mustered a deputation to go to Dorchester and persuade the Southampton & Dorchester committee to build the line along a costal route serving Wareham and Poole, rather than the original proposal for an inland route from Wimborne via Bloxworth and Bere Regis. John Hales Calcraft was requested to present the petition to the next meeting of the Southampton & Dorchester board in Dorchester: he was unable to do so in person but added his name to support of the petition.

William Pike stated in the meeting the ease of laying a railway across the Dorset heathland as better than any other county in his experience (having engineered and built his own gravity-worked line from Furzebrook to Ridge Wharf about 1840).

John Hales Calcraft was a powerful Purbeck landowner (including most of the town of Wareham) and MP. for Wareham

during the 1870s and William Pike, of Pike Brothers Co., was his political assistant and a fellow landowner at Furzebrook. In 1825 Calcraft's father, John Calcraft, had promoted the Dorset and Somerset Canal and Railway Company's line to Poole, with a branch line to Wareham. (Some years earlier, in Paris during the early 1820s, John H. Calcraft had had an affair with Princess Pauline Bonaparte - Napoleon's sister, but this did not seem to prejudice his political career, as later he was MP for Wareham up to 1881!)

Thus it can be seen that the two largest clay producers in Purbeck managed to bring the Southampton & Dorchester railway to Wareham as a railhead for the Purbeck district, although their own mines were not to be connected directly to the system for another four decades.

John Scott, 1st Lord Eldon of Encombe was a Tory MP and when visiting his estate from London it used to take three days to make the journey prior to the opening of the railways. It is no wonder the aristocracy were keen to see a rail connection to London pass close to their estates.

On 25 March 1845 Grissell & Peto took out a two-year lease on part of the Ballast Quay in Hamworthy, this after negotiation with Richard Pinney of Poole Corporation. This land was to be used for storage of materials to construct the Southampton & Dorchester Railway. So it was that the first consignment of rails were landed from a schooner at Richard Pinney's own shipyard on 9 April 1845. The rails are thought to have come from South Wales via Cardiff: according to the shipping movements. J. J. Guest's Dowlais Iron Works had supplied the London & Southampton with rail in 1835 and track spikes in 1840, although no records have been found for supply of rails to the Southampton & Dorchester railway yet. The railway mania of the 1840s had caused a sharp rise in the cost of, as well as shortages of, rail in Britain, so Peto had been wise to stockpile rail in advance of starting the civil engineering works.

Following the bankruptcy of his shipyard in 1848, Richard Pinney had became the manager of the Southampton & Dorchester Railway Wharf in Hamworthy by July 1848. This wharf was constructed by J.J. Guest of Canford on his land, as Poole Council were unable to release the land next to the station due to an ongoing legal battle with Mr. Parr.

By 1881 Richard Pinney's son, Richard Edward Pinney, had become mines manager at Norden, possibly through contacts with his fellow councillor George Penney, the Poole agent for B. Fayle & Co. By the turn of the century R. E. Pinney was trading as B. Fayle & Co., so presumably owned the company.

In October 1847 Thomas Phippard, the Wareham solicitor and Clerk of the Wareham and Purbeck Turnpike, proposed a branch line to Swanage from the Southampton and Dorchester at Wareham and the line was duly surveyed.

Like William Pitt, Phippard also saw Swanage as becoming a popular seaside resort, and could pick up trade from holidaymakers, as well as the trade in clay and stone from the area. Thomas Phippard was also married into the Brown family, who owned the Furzebrook estate and leased out the clay mines within the estate.

An initial meeting of the promoters of the Swanage Railway was held on 23 October 1847 and included William Joseph Pike, Thomas Phippard, Freeland Filliter and Joseph Willis from Norden amongst their numbers. The promoters achieved the approval of the scheme with most of the significant landowners of the area such as George Bankes, John Calcraft and the second Lord Eldon. Obviously Lord Eldon did not share his grandfather's views about the development of Swanage as a seaside town, as he purchased much of William Pitt's land in Swanage including the prestigious Victoria hotel. He also promoted a scheme to build a large dock and canal at Wareham in November 1848, although nothing ever became of the scheme; due to being his declared of unsound mind in June 1851.

Sadly nothing came of the first Swanage Railway proposal, at this time due mainly to the slump in railway share prices. There was also some opposition to the railway scheme by Swanage traders, as they were operating the Truck system at that time and saw the proposed railway as a threat to their trading restrictions.

In 1861 there was an attempt by the LSWR to sanction a branch from Worgret to Creech Heath, but little else appears known of this proposal. Either the LSWR were worried about the competition stealing the clay traffic, or the merchants and landowners were prepared to offer private sponsorship to serve their own purposes, as an amendment was issued in 1863 with the addition of a tramway to Ridge. This latter amendment was only two years before Pike's tramway from Furzebrook to Ridge was rebuilt to take steam traction.

The Purbeck Ball Clay Mines

Ball clay had been dug in Devon and Dorset since the 16th Century, at that time mainly for production of clay tobacco pipes, but by the mid-18th Century new production methods by potters such as Josiah Wedgwood had increased this demand. The fine ball clays of these areas were now being used to mass produce white-bodied tableware which was being exported all over the world.

In 1669 ball clay was being shipped from Russell Point, Arne and Thomas Hyde established a Quay in this area in 1768. By 1793 Hyde was declared bankrupt and the key landowners, John Calcraft and William Moreton Pitt, formed a consortium to produce ball clay. Liverpool shipping agent Mr. Barker Chifney was appointed as their agent in 1792. In 1803 Chifney's financial backer, Richard Rivers, died and he was made bankrupt. The agency for the Dorset clay pits was then taken over in October 1803 by the London-based merchant and shipping insurer, Benjamin Fayle & Co.

Ball clay production in the late 18th Century was mainly in open-cast pits, the clay being transported to the nearest navigable waterway by means of pack horse. This was far from ideal, as on a good day a pack horse could carry two to four hundredweight. of clay, whilst on a wet day the horse might sink in the soft ground and bring the whole operation to a standstill. The

Above - *Fayle's Offices and Smithy about 1900.*
Opposite page - *Map of Middlebere Plateway and Fayle's Tramway.*

roads of the time were in a poor state and the same fate would have befallen any cart trying to transport clay during the winter months. Also the road from the pits at Norden ran to Wareham Quay, which was only small and at the end of a long winding channel at the back of Poole Harbour.

During the Napoleonic wars, it was said that the young sea-faring men of Poole and Wareham used to hide in the clay pits, to avoid the notorious press gangs 'recruiting' for the Royal Navy.

The Napoleonic wars had caused a sharp increase in the price of horse fodder and thus transportation costs. There was also a general recession in British manufacturing industry, due to the difficulty of importing and exporting goods to the European continent from Britain. This was especially so in the pottery industry, thus there was urgent need to reduce production costs. Increasing the efficiency of the ball clay industry supplying the potteries was one way to achieve this.

Following the defeat of the French fleet at Trafalgar, the coastal waters of Britain were once again rendered safe for merchant shipping, although British exports were still restricted to the foreign ports that Napoleon had not blockaded.

With the prospect of British industry recovering from recession and the promise of increased efficiency, it was decided to build a 'railroad' to transport ball clay from the Norden pits near Corfe Castle, to Middlebere Quay at the back of Poole Harbour. A canal would have been too expensive to construct whilst there was also the lack of a suitable water supply at the Norden

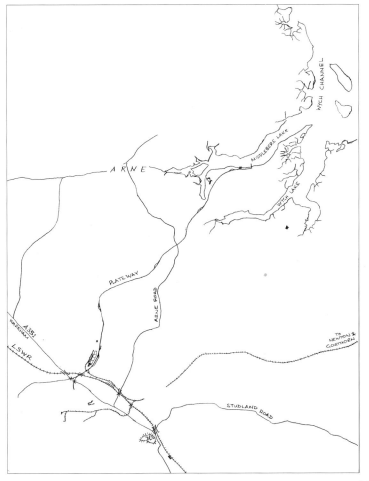

end of the line, therefore a Plateway was the obvious choice to solve the transport problems.

There are several possibilities as to who instigated building of the Middlebere Plateway, but we do know it was financed by B. Fayle & Co. One possibility is that William Moreton Pitt was in dire financial straits by 1805 and was looking for ways to increase the returns from his estate. The Pitt family already had 80 years of experience with railways from their colliery in Tanfield, Durham (just a few miles from George Stephenson's birthplace) and perhaps this is what inspired the building of the plateway.

It is also thought that Benjamin Fayle was taking great interest in the new Surrey Iron Railway being built along the Wandle valley, only a few miles from his London home, as the Middlebere Plateway shared the same construction techniques as the Surrey railway. The third possibility is Josiah Wedgwood, already a shareholder in the Monmouth Canal Co., who had employed Benjamin Outram and John Hodgkinson to construct the Sirhowy Tramroad in the years immediately before the commissioning of the Middlebere line. Wedgwood's successors may have seen the advantages offered by the Sirhowy Tramroad and thought they should apply this technology to their ball clay suppliers.

Whoever it was, in August 1806 the Middlebere Plateway opened to traffic and became the first horse-drawn iron railway system in Dorset and also one of the first in the South West. Opening of the Middlebere Plateway more than halved the number of men and horses needed to transport the clay from the pits to the quayside.

Elsewhere in the West Country, several inclined planes had already been built by the canal companies in North Somerset and Bath by 1806, but these were generally quite short, and relied on gravity for operation. Ralph Allen of Prior Park, Bath had constructed his wooden waggonway in 1730, to serve his stone quarries at Coombe Down. This used cast iron wheels, but still relied on wooden rails, as iron rails did not come into use in Britain until 1787.

The Middlebere Plateway

When it opened (by 16 August 1806), there were huge redundancies as well as increased production, Fayle's workforce falling from 250 men in 1805 to only 110 in 1809. According to one source, production increased from 14,500 tons of ball clay in 1802 to 22,000 tons in 1808, although these figures do seem rather high for the general trend in production at the time.

Benjamin Outram, the canal & tramway engineer, had adopted the iron plateway system in 1795 for mineral tramway construction, which replaced the traditional methods in the north-east of using wooden rails with flanged wheels. By 1806 this system of construction was still popular, although cast iron bulb rail in cast iron chairs with flanged wheels was being used on some tramways. Wrought iron rails were not available at that period, but when they appeared in 1812 they were double the cost of cast iron plates.

Early wrought iron rails had a tendency to wear quickly compared to the cast iron plates, as a form of chill casting gave the plates a hardened running surface. Once the hardened surface of the cast iron plates wore through, subsequent wear was rapid and resulted in a groove forming in the running surface of the plate.

The Middlebere Plateway was constructed by John Hodgkinson, cousin and colleague of Benjamin Outram. Hodgkinson used 3ft. 6in. gauge on the Hay Railway, the Cheltenham & Gloucester Railway, the Forest of Dean, and some of his other projects. The Middlebere plateway gauge is quoted as 3ft. 9in. in some sources, and is drawn approximating to this gauge on the Swanage Railway bridge plans, although measurements taken of surviving sleeper pairs indicate a gauge of 3ft. 6in. It is also possible that the gauge spread over its 100 year existence, as occurred on some other well used plateways.

Outram himself favoured a 4ft 2in gauge for plateway construction, in order to allow hogshead casks and other bulky items to be loaded width-wise into the wagons, and this was the gauge used on public lines such as the Surrey Iron Railway and the Sirhowy Tramroad.

The construction of Middlebere was similar to that of the Surrey Iron Railway, although detail differences existed in the design of the plates and spikes. The SIR cast iron plates used a significant toe-in on the vertical flanges and local thickening of the horizontal flange, to give a Z-section between the stone sleepers in Outram's design. The Middlebere plates were of uniform thickness with the flanges set almost at right angles, similar to the plates used in the Forest of Dean.

The completed line was 3½ miles long, of single track with three passing loops, and cost £2,000 per mile to construct. This investment enabled the clay to be shipped from the pits to the Quayside for 6d per ton.

A number of pits were served on either side of the Wareham to Corfe road from where the line ran across Middlebere heath on a gradual falling gradient of 1 in 150 to 1 in 180, to arrive at the quay on Middlebere Creek.

Shallow cuttings and embankments were required across the heath land and a tunnel under the main road was built in 1807, to serve the clay pits already in use on the west of the road. Two tunnels appear to have been built in the cuttings formed by the original pits which straddled the turnpike road, with the south tunnel providing a loop from the pits to the weathering beds. The track layout in the pits area was changed frequently, as the workings moved southward and westward from the original site.

The south tunnel was rebuilt in 1848 to gain access to a new pit to the south of the original workings. This new pit was in the path of the old turnpike road, which was re-aligned a few

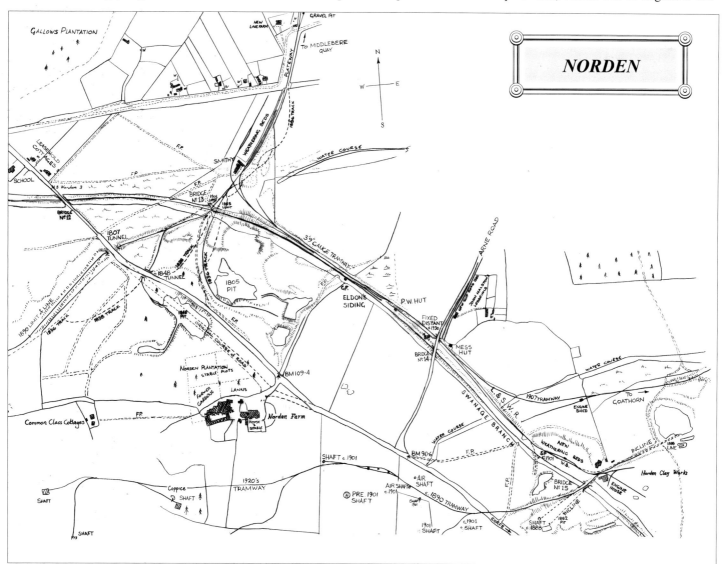

Above - The West End of the North tunnel, built in 1807, and passing under the present day A351.

Right - The West End of the South tunnel passing under the present day A351. This tunnel was rebuilt in 1848.

yards eastward to facilitate the new excavation. Originally laid in a loop, the 1848 rebuild split the track into two separate lines, each serving a different pit.

The junction east of the tunnels was also moved closer to the tunnels, leaving the original line to the south pit as a siding. Eventually the track was reduced back to just the single northern line by the time the Swanage Railway was built, as these pits were by then disused. The keystone of each tunnel was inscribed with 'BF.' and the date, 1807 for the North and 1848 on the South tunnel. The various sidings into the pits all converged at the smithy, where the company office and carpentry shop were also located: this was adjacent to the clay weathering beds.

A platform was provided at the weathering beds to aid loading and unloading the clay. Once weathered, the clay was taken to Middlebere Quay where it was loaded into small sailing vessels for shipment to Poole Quay, then transferred to sea going vessels for shipment to the potteries. At New Line Farm, just

A plateway train at the weathering beds by New Line Farm.

North of the Smithy, a siding was provided serving a gravel pit, presumably a source of the track ballast for the Plateway.

At Middlebere Quay there were various sidings serving a pier and a slipway. A large, thatched, stone, clay storage 'cellar' and several small buildings existed along the Quay and on one, a flagstaff was provided. The flagstaff was thought to be for signalling the shipping movements at the Quayside, as a similar arrangement was made at Goathorn pier in later years. Perhaps the idea of signal flags at Middlebere Quay and Newton came from the Napoleonic signal posts at Ballard Down and St Aldhams Head. Some years ago a ring of stone sleepers and a pivot stone was unearthed on the quay itself, which could have been the base of a crane or windlass. This has since been covered over again. R.W. Kidner also states there was a turntable in use on the quay although this is not shown on a 1901 Ordnance Survey map.

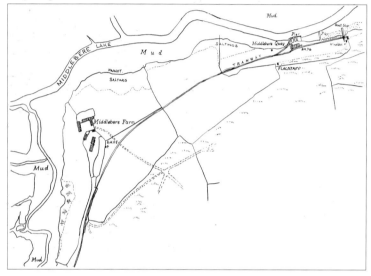

Map of Middlebere Quay c.1901.

In 1812 Middlebere Creek, or Middlebere Lake to use the Dorset terminology, was navigable by vessels of 30 tons. Progressive silting up of Poole Harbour now makes access to the Quay even by rowing boat a challenge.

When working, each train consisted of five two-ton wagons hauled by two or three horses with one groom in charge. This replaced the equivalent of over 60 packhorses with their requisite number of grooms. In 1805 the inventory of the works shows that Fayle & Co. had two 10 ton boats and one 15 ton boat, as in 1812 three 10 ton trains per day from Norden to Middlebere

were sufficient to transport about 10,000 tons per annum to the quay for shipping to the potteries.

The construction of the Plateway was similar to the Surrey Iron Railway, and used cast iron plates secured to Purbeck stone sleepers, set in gravel ballast, a single iron spike in an oak plug securing two plates. The plates were 3ft long with 3in vertical flanges, and weighed about 40 lb each. The sleepers were 12 to 15in long by 14 to 19in wide and weigh 60 to 70 lb each. One of the surviving plates shows a groove in the bottom flange which was thought to be wear from the wagon wheels, but a similar plateway in Bude was said to have had grooves cast in the plates from new in order to reduce chafing of the vertical flanges.

It is not known exactly how the points were arranged at Middlebere, but the Haytor and Bude plateways used a pivoted section vertical flange where lines split in order to guide the wheels in the right direction. The later Fayle's tramway used stub points extensively and it is thought that this may have been a continuation of practice from the plateway, whereby the section of rails where the track divides are pivoted at one end and are moved between the two diverging sections of track at the other end.

The rolling stock consisted of 4-wheel, wooden bodied wagons fitted with Collinge's patent axle (as given in Farey's General View of Agriculture in Derbyshire: 1817): similar to some of the Bodmin and Wadebridge wagons, where the wheels rotate on a fixed axle. The most important features of the Collinge axle, was a means of positive lubrication with a hub cap to prevent dirt ingress and a thrust bearing at the inner and outer ends of the journal allowing the gauge to be accurately maintained. (John Collinge had a foundry in Westminster Bridge Road, near the approach to Waterloo Station and was a prolific inventor with many patents to his name. Spherical bearing door hinges were another invention of his, some of which can be seen at Kingston Lacy House and also on almost every Bulleid and BR Mk.1 carriage door.) His patent axle was used on most passenger-carrying horse carriages

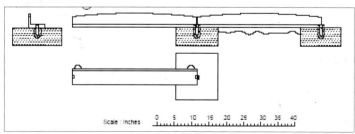

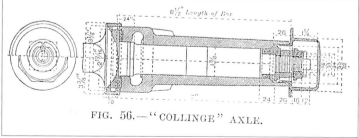

Above - Drawing of Middlebere Plateway track.
Middle right - Platway point at Bleanavon Ironworks.

Collinge Patent Axletree.

Above - *Coalbrookdale* cast iron plateway wheels at Ironbridge Gorge museum.

Right - *Middlebere Plateway model.*

Bottom - *Tiny' at Goathorn.*

from 1792 onwards and enabled the use of high speed stage coaches over long distances without continual maintenance to the bearings.)

The wagon bodies were probably made of elm, as this was the preferred timber due to its durability and ease of cutting into wide planks. External iron strapping was used to prevent contamination of the clay. A drop door was provided at the Quayside end of the wagons and unloading was probably by up-ending each wagon in turn at the end of the pier where there was a portal frame with a block and tackle for attachment of a winch hook to the back of the wagon.

The wagon wheelbase was approximately 3 ft., as this spread the weight over two rail plates each side. Coupling bars were provided on the outside of the dumb buffers, with a two-hook and one-link coupling on each side of the wagon. The horse harness was attached to the leading wagon at the same points. The wagon wheels were of cast iron construction, with eight spokes and an extended hub to accommodate the Collinge's patent axle and thus maintain the correct gauge. Similar wheels but without the Collinge axletree, were used on the Dean forest plateways, and at Coalbrookdale, where they were cast by the local ironworks. Both original and recently cast replica examples can be seen at the Ironbridge and Blists Hill museums.

Throughout the life of the Plateway, traction was by means of horses, except for the rumour of the trial run of a Lewin-built engine 'Corfe' (later known as 'Tiny') when

delivered some time between 1868 and 1874. The results of this trial were a series of cracked plates and the engine was taken to the new pits at Newton where edge rail was used instead of plates. Presumably the engine was originally supplied with flangeless wheels, which is possible as Lewin had supplied other customers with engines of this type.

In May 1854 B. Fayle & Co. opened up extensive new pits at Newton and a rail link was provided to Goathorn Peninsula with a pier leading to the South Deep channel in Poole Harbour. This system was probably laid as edge rail, and must have been 3' 9" gauge by the 1870s upon the arrival of the Lewin engine from Poole Foundry.

Although Goathorn pier itself dates from 1854, quays were in use at Ower, Goathorn and Redhorn by 1846, as a letter to John Hales Calcraft was sent by Poole Corporation warning of the effect on the South Deep by the scouring of Poole Harbour entrance by the steam tug 'Lioness' hired from Newcastle. These quays are shown on the 1849 Admiralty map of the harbour, but without the pier at Goathorn.

In 1875 new pits were opened up at Matchams, about ½ mile south east of the existing workings at Norden. These were also provided with a 3ft. 0in. gauge tramway leading back to the weathering beds at the smithy. It is thought that this rail link was laid with edge rail, as no evidence of stone sleepers has been found and a contemporary engraving in Robinson's 'Picturesque Rambles in the Isle of Purbeck', 1882, shows railway-style wagons on a double track incline with conventional cross-tie sleepers. This tramway was a rope-hauled incline into the two pits either side of the Swanage Branch, being powered by a stationary engine on the high ground on the East side of Bridge 15. Double track was laid on the incline to enable empty wagons going down to counter-balance full wagons being hauled up from the bottom of the pits. The 1885 bridge plans for the Swanage Railway show the incline increased to 3 tracks of 3ft 0in gauge flat bottom rail.

This short length of tramway was used independently to convey clay from the new pits to the weathering beds, the weathered clay then being transferred to the plateway for shipment to Middlebere. When the Swanage Railway opened, Bridge No. 15 was provided to carry the inclined tramway across the railway cutting and was constructed from poured concrete with RSJ and timber decking.

The LSWR Swanage Branch.

Several attempts to build a branch line from Wareham to Swanage had been thwarted since 1847, but in May 1885 the branch line to Swanage was finally opened, taking an avoiding route around the outskirts of Wareham and crossing both rail systems; of Pike Brothers at Furzebrook and B. Fayle & Co. at Norden. Exchange sidings were then provided at each location to enable shipment of ball clay by the LSWR to the potteries in the North. The siding for Fayle & Co. was provided shortly after the opening of the line, but Pike Brothers were not served by the LSWR until after the turn of the century. A report at the opening of the line, suggests that Pike's clay would be transported by rail from Furzebrook to Hamworthy Ballast Quay and not direct by rail to Staffordshire as had been envisaged in the earlier 1847 promotion of the Swanage Railway.

The Swanage branch diverged from the Southampton and Dorchester at Worgret Junction, thence south-east towards Corfe Castle, crossing the Pike Brothers tramway at Furzebrook over Bridge No.11. On Sunday 7 September 1884 about 40 navvies diverted Pike's tramway from its original straight course, to curve towards Furzebrook House in order to pass beneath the Swanage Railway which was under construction. By Monday morning the tramway was fully functional again.

After passing under what is now the A351, the line swings round to follow the road into Corfe, running parallel to Fayle's tramway between the Smithy and the new pits at Matchams. An exchange siding was provided one mile North of Corfe Castle station, called Eldon's Siding, after Lord Eldon of Encombe who owned the land. At the South end of this siding, the Arne road passes over the LSWR on bridge No. 14, which is of Purbeck stone construction. Adjacent to this, a similar bridge was provided for passage of the tramway, presumably built at the same time, as the road was elevated by the Swanage Railway Company in order to pass over bridge 14.

LSWR instruction No. 206 of 1898, details the transition from Train Staff and Ticket to Tyer's Train Tablet System to commence on Sunday 18 September. Under the new system the ground frame at Eldon's Siding was locked, and could be released by the tablet from Corfe Castle. SR instruction No. 14 of 1929 details the removal of the shelter and ground signal at Eldon's Siding. During the Second World War a gun emplacement siding was laid on the up side, parallel to Eldon's Siding. This was removed in 1946, but the anchor chain and block are still in the undergrowth today.

To the North of Eldon's Siding, the LSWR passes over the Middlebere plateway on bridge No. 13, which is a single span archway of brick construction. The archway through which the Plateway passed is tapered, to allow for passage of a re-aligned plateway junction, with the point positioned under the bridge. The original line to the south pit had been truncated to a siding on the east side of bridge 13 by 1886 and was probably never re-laid under the bridge. A diverted footpath heading south and crossing the plateway under the bridge was in use at the turn of the century. From what information is available on maps and via a report of the opening of the line, it appears that the plateway to the South tunnel under the road was disused by 1885 and only the North tunnel line to the western pits remained in use. By 1882 it is possible that this line was only used for backfilling the old pits with spoil, as the tramway line from the new pits was laid across the top of the old plateway, bisecting the Plateway line between the Smithy and bridge 13.

To the south of Eldon's siding, Fayle's tramway crosses the LSWR on a unique skew arch bridge (Bridge No. 15), which was built by E. G. Perkins of Lymington using concrete retaining walls with a braced steel joist and timber deck which crosses on a down gradient towards Corfe Castle. The three track tramway may have been laid across the bridge initially, but by 1888 a single line on a curve ran across the bridge and down toward a shaft at the bottom of the old open cast workings. By 1901 the bridge had been levelled by dumping spoil on top of the wooden decking and a single track line was laid

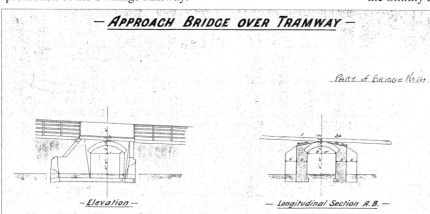

Bridge 14 (Fayle's tramway) works drawing.

30

to serve the new pits on the West of the main road. These pits had been opened up just before the turn of the century, a few yards south of the Norden Farm buildings. In 1938 the old bridge decking was found to be rotten, and a new centre span was laid using two rolled steel joists on a level 3ft 9in wide pitch, but retained the original outer spans. This bridge now forms the centre piece of the new Purbeck Mineral and Mining Museum currently being built at the Norden park and ride site of the Swanage Railway.

Between 1905 and 1907, Benjamin Fayle & Co. built a new line from Norden to connect with their Newton works line, serving Goathorn Pier, presumably re-gauging the old Matchams tramway at the same time.

This now provided a through connection from the pits at Norden to Poole Harbour via a 3ft. 9in. gauge edge-rail system equipped with the steam locomotive 'Tiny'. 'Tiny' was soon supplemented by a re-gauged second hand Manning Wardle from the Thames Water Works in 1909. This marked the end for the Middlebere plateway and the line closed around this time, partially due to being outdated and worn out, and partially due to the continued silting up of Poole Harbour restricting the size of vessels able to navigate Middlebere Lake.

The track of the plateway was lifted shortly after closure, possibly for the iron during the First World War, and all that remains are the ballast and a few stone sleepers. Most of the line is still accessible as it is now National Trust land and is used as a path to Middlebere Farm from the Arne road.

One item of note was in 1907, when Fayle & Co. spent a large sum of money to renew their connection with Poole Harbour rather than let the LSWR transport their clay to exactly the same destination, Poole Quay. It is possible that U-Boat activity during the First World War persuaded the clay companies of the Purbecks that rail is safer, as Goathorn Pier was derelict by the mid 1930s and all the clay was being transported by rail. Pike Brothers continued to use Ridge Wharf until the Second World War, when the military commandeered the wharf. From then on Pike Brothers used the Furzebrook sidings to dispatch their wares.

During the 1950s road transport became more affordable, and by 1970 all the tramways had closed. Furzebrook sidings remained in use after the closure of the Swanage Branch in 1972, but eventually gave way to road haulage in the 1980s.

During the 1960s an M7 collided with one of the lorries loading clay at the under bridge where the present day Norden station entrance is located. Luckily the M7 wasn't damaged! The Swanage Railway achieved its rebirth in 1974 with the creation of the preservation company which managed to save the line from destruction, and now it is the turn of the clay tramways of the Purbecks.

A few years ago a small group formed the Purbeck Mineral and Mining Group, whose aim was to build a working museum to the area's industry adjacent to Norden station. Land has been acquired at Norden and planning permission obtained to build the museum. Several of the old mine buildings from Norden Farm and some of the underground rolling stock have been donated by Imerys, the successors to ECC., Pike Brothers, B. Fayle & Co. The locomotive *Secundus* and one of Pike Brother's wagons have been loaned to the museum, and are on display at Corfe and Norden respectively. The old mine foreman's hut has

Above - *Bridge No. 14 (Fayle's Tramway)*
Below - *Bridge No 14 (Swanage Railway) Arne Road.*

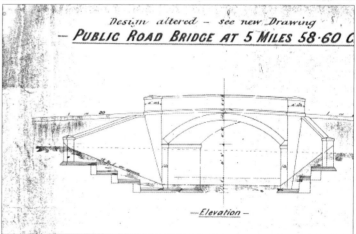

been restored and transported to Norden, but now the race is on to finish the trans-shipment shed at Norden in order to be able to open the museum to the public.

If anyone has any memories or photographs of the Purbeck clay mines, or who fancies lending a hand to help create the museum, all would be most gratefully received.

Working parties are on site at Norden on Wednesdays and Sundays.

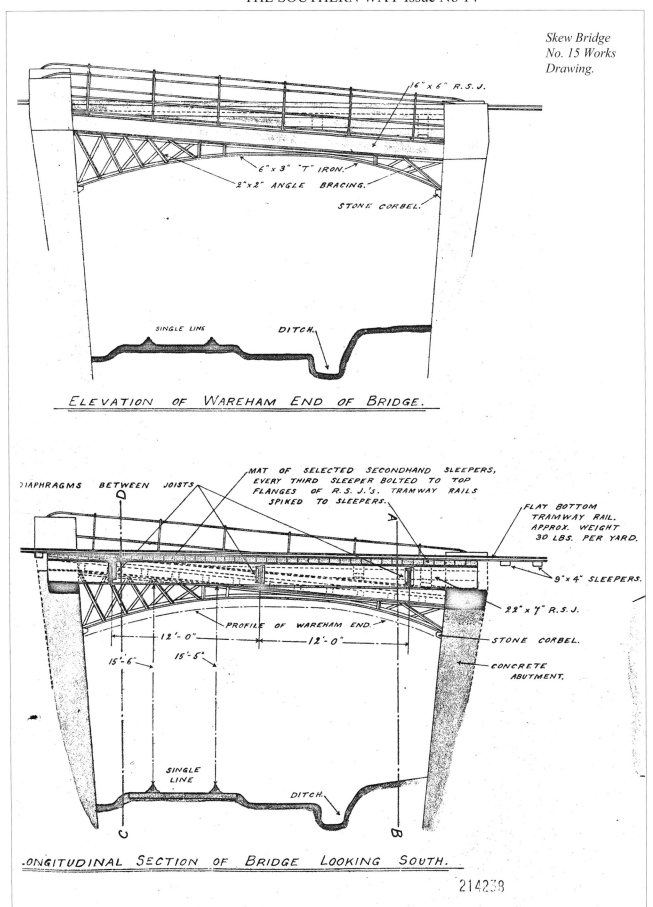

Skew Bridge No. 15 Works Drawing.

ELEVATION OF WAREHAM END OF BRIDGE.

LONGITUDINAL SECTION OF BRIDGE LOOKING SOUTH.

Right - *'Tiny' on the new line to Newton.*

Centre left - *View above skew arch Bridge No. 15.*

Centre right - *PMMMG Museum at Norden (ex-mine Foreman's Hut*

Eldon's siding in the late 1960's looking towards Corfe. Left is the entrance gate to the siding which was interlocked to the ground frame, right is he fixed distant signal near Bridge 14, and the whistle sign for the occupation crossing before Corfe viaduct.

ASHFORD WINTER 1962/3

By Dave Hammersley

No. 31271 Ashford Shed 24 February 1963

The winter of 1962 / 63 was the most severe experienced in Britain for 200 years. East Kent, jutting out into the North Sea and the English Channel, was exposed to the worst of the Northerly winds, which whipped up the snow into great drifts.

The railways of the area suffered immensely, but having recently been electrified and dieselised, had no locomotives suitable for the bufferbeam mounted snowploughs of the era. No loco propelled ploughs had yet been built for the D6500 series 'Cromptons'. Fortunately Ashford Works had held on to three 'C' class 0-6-0s for shunting, and these were pressed into service clearing the tracks of Kent from their base in the old steam shed at Ashford.

We caught up with them in January 1963, when the worst of the weather had abated and travel once more had some certainty of getting home again. Snow was still on the ground and the locos were standing ready in light steam. It was a bleak sight, with only three steam locos simmering in a large shed yard which only months before had been packed with engines of all sizes.

Above - Left to right numbers Nos. 31280, 31271 and 31592 stand outside Ashford shed building with snowploughs attached. Seen between them is a spare plough propped up on its support legs. By this time the only other occupants were diesel shunters for the yards and a handful of D6500 series 'Cromptons', now better known as Class 33. 6 January 1963

Below - No. 31280 waits for more snow. In the background is the driving trailer from push-pull set No. 660. 6 January 1963.

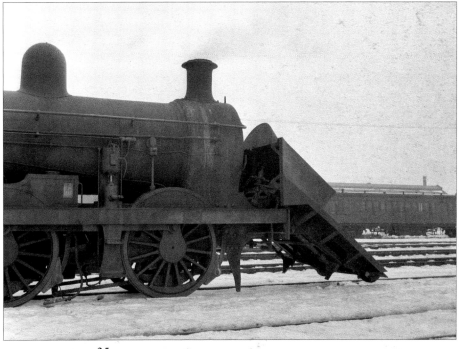

Above - rear view of No. 31592, seen at the end of February, shows the construction of the Southern Regions' standard snow-plough. The loco buffers were removed and the plough bolted on using the same holes. Vertical adjustment was made with the handwheel above the footplate where a special, triangular bracket was fixed to the mainframes. The bracket itself stayed on the loco and pivoted on the frames to rest flush with the plating. The plough is seen in its travelling position, well clear of the track. In action, the bottom will be much closer to the rails. When it is not needed, the hinged legs are folded down and the plough left standing in a back corner of the shed. At the top is the half cone which protects the smokebox from the force of the snow when ploughing. Just visible is the catch allowing this part to be hinged away to allow the smokebox door to be opened. Later these ploughs were mounted on the back of redundant Schools class tenders to be propelled by diesel locos. 24 February 1963.

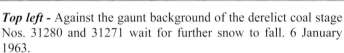

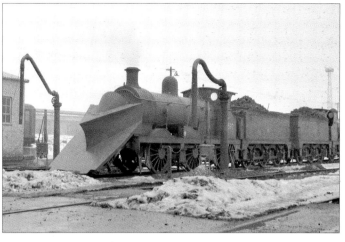

Top left - Against the gaunt background of the derelict coal stage Nos. 31280 and 31271 wait for further snow to fall. 6 January 1963.

Bottom - *No.* 31280 waits in front of the shed. As well as the snowplough she also has de-icing gear fitted between the leading axleboxes of the tender. Another non-standard fitting is the Westinghouse air pump mounted on the footplate ahead of the cab, probably to power the de-icing gear. Several C class had been Westinghouse fitted from the start to work LCDR and other air braked stock, but No. 31280 was not recorded as being one of them. 6 January 1963.

Top right - A pile of cleared snow stands in front of No. 31592, now preserved in SECR finery on the Bluebell Railway, but here seen in scruffy BR black with a tender full of coal and smoke drifting gently from the chimney.

As the Bluebell has one of these ploughs mounted on a Schools class tender we could see it restored to original condition and attached to No. (31)592 again for a unique reminder of how winters used to be. 6 January 1963.

Right - By the end of February the snow had cleared, but the trusty 'C' class were still standing ready with snowploughs attached and were even seen shunting Ashford Works with them. No. 31592 is silhouetted against the chilly Kent skyline. 24 February 1963.

Bottom - Six weeks earlier the threat of snow was still very real as No. 31280 stands in the shed yard. No. 31271 on the right still has snow on its blade and a spare plough stands at the rear. In better weather they were stored at the inner ends of the shed roads or on the track which extended out through the opposite end of the shed alongside the entrance path. 6 January 1963.

Opposite page, top - *Nos.* 31271 and 31592 stand in the yard while No. 31280 is silhouetted deep inside the shed, outside the foreman's office. 24 February 1963.

Opposite page, bottom - In the background are the storage tanks for the new diesel locos and the rail tanks which supplied them.

Nos. 31271 and 31280 did not survive, but probably many of their parts live on in preserved loco 31592. One of them was used as a stationary boiler in the Kimberley Wagon Works and certainly donated its chimney! 24 February 1963.

The first in this sequence of pictures, moving from west to east, shows No. 34080 74 Squadron approaching Exeter St Davids from Cowley Bridge Junction with a train from the North Devon Line. Unseen, but roughly behind the cab, a banking engine (or may be two) will be standing waiting to come on the back of what seems to be a fairly long train. From the train the passengers will be able to see a variety of sidings serving industries and warehouses to the right of the bracket signals. It was not un-usual to see vehicles being moved here by hand power, with the shunter using a pinch bar to get a vehicle in motion before pushing it along with a hand on the buffer. On one occasion in the late 1950s, a very smart gentleman in full uniform and a clearly new brimmed hat with gold braid was seen pushing a BR goods van in such a way: complete with a piece of paper to keep his hands clean.

40

THE EXETER BANK

Maurice Hopper and Stuart Kerslake
Photographs by Philip Conolly

The LSWR arrived in Exeter from the east in 1860. Its station in Queen Street was close to the city centre but well above the level of the River Exe. St Davids Station had been built next to the river by the Bristol and Exeter Railway, which had arrived in Exeter from the north, by way of the Culm and Exe Valleys in 1844. To provide a connection to its furthest outpost in the west, the Bodmin and Wadebridge Railway, and to gain access to Plymouth and North Devon, the South Western had to cross both the River Exe and what was now the Great Western mainline. To do this, a steep bank with a gradient of 1 in 37 was constructed between Exeter's two main stations, partly in a tunnel through St Davids Hill. Thus was created a short piece of railway, low on economy but high in operational interest. It is hoped some of this interest is illustrated by the following selection of pictures from a collection of Philip Conolly's photographs.

At one time the Southern Railway considered the idea of building a flyover for its trains to cross the Great Western mainline and so avoid conflicting movements during busy periods at St Davids. Had this plan had been carried out, an additional benefit would have been to shorten the length of the steep gradient, the Southern lines being kept high enough to cross the south end of the simplified St Davids trackwork to reach a high level platform between the station and the locomotive shed. The junction between the two routes would have been to the north of the station and the Red Cow level crossing, in the vicinity of the Riverside Yard.

One of Exmouth Junction's Z Class engines, No. 30952 and an unidentified Mogul at the head of an up freight train. There will also be a banker on the rear. As the 'board' is off we can assume the conversation of whistles has taken place and that shortly the train will be pounding through St Davids Tunnel, out of sight but still in hearing. To the right Alice Conolly's shadow on Platform 1 tells us this is possibly the 1.15pm transfer freight from Riverside Yard to Exmouth Junction. To the left a former Great Western passenger van seems to have been dropped off the back of an up Western Region train at the south end of platform 5.

Above - *West Country No. 34108 Wincanton and BR Mk1 4-Car Set 516, with a green Maunsell insert, has the road with a long up train, the head code suggesting the Summer Saturday through train from Plymouth to Waterloo. Apart from the 'Brighton' (the daily Plymouth to Brighton train) it was only Summer Saturday trains that were this length on the Waterloo services at St Davids. Most Southern passenger services passing through St Davids were relatively short formations, being portions that were formed into longer trains at Exeter Central for the journey to London. The Southern's requirement for at least two paths through St Davids for every express working for both up and down trains, while reducing the loads, added to the complications of working the bank. To the left, hidden behind the support for the signal gantry and obscured by steam, appears to be a chimney of a Mogul or a Z Class and the end of a coach. Perhaps a down train has just arrived with a loco at the back that will be dropped off here to run forward on to the spur at Red Cow Crossing to await another banking duty.*

Opposite top *- Light Pacific No. 34080 74 Squadron pulls out of Exeter St Davids with an up train for Exeter Central. The portions that made up the London trains arrived with a head code for Exeter Central rather than for Waterloo. As it comes out of the shadow of the canopy on Platform 3 the first coach, a BR Mk1, displays its crimson and cream livery.*

Opposite bottom - *West Country Class No. 34030 Watersmeet is committed to the climb as it turns on to the up Waterloo line on leaving Platform 3 at St Davids. Again the head code tells us the train is going to Exeter Central.*

The Appendix to the Working Timetable (1960) states, "The maximum single engine load is 200 tons for West Country and Battle of Britain locomotives. An assisting engine or engines to be provided when the weight of the train exceeds the hauling capacity of the train engine. Assisting engines (at front or rear if the load is not more than 200 tons and at the rear if over 200 tons) to be provided, the type of assisting engine to be determined by adding together the hauling capacity of the train engine and the assisting engine."

Top - An Exmouth Junction M7 No. 30374 regains level ground as it crosses the down Western Region lines to the West. The roof of the West Box can be seen over the third and fourth containers. The single disc in front of the chimney is the indication for the North Devon Line, but it is more likely with this motive power that it is only going as far as Riverside Yard on a transfer freight. This would have been the site of the possible flyover if the Southern had felt it a worthwhile investment.

Bottom - Here M7 No. 30374 is led by its fellow Exmouth Junction engine Z Class No. 30951 towards Exeter St Davids. Following the steel sided open are three 'Pallvans'. These were an attempt to provide modern goods handling methods using fork lift trucks. However they were still hampered by their overall size being smaller than contemporary road vehicles, a factor which reduced an economic advantage. By this time pallet-carrying vehicles in Europe were at least twice as long making a 50% saving on running gear equipment and maintenance. However, yards such as those at the top of the bank with its wagon turntables would never have been able to accommodate such long vehicles and so the railway continued, paralysed by the lack of investment required in the infrastructure to develop economic services.

Opposite - This picture of N Class No. 31843 on the 11.47 Exeter Central, all stations to Plymouth Friary, shows perhaps better than any other the rate at which the line dropped down from Exeter Central to St Davids. It clearly illustrates the need for a clear path to platform 4 at the latter station to be established before the down starter could be pulled at the Central. This requirement did not endear the Southern to the Western, as these moves effectively occupied the Western's mainline to the West for about five minutes. The level tracks to the right are the access to the down carriage sidings, referred to as 'The Field', and to the left a single carriage siding occupied by a Maunsell set. Behind this was a siding with wagon turntables giving access to a range of builders' materials and timber yards, which was also sometimes used as a carriage siding. The siding between the coaches and the ganger standing in the 'six foot' was a catch road ending in a buffer stop set against the embankment wall.

Opposite top - A similar pairing to that seen earlier of Z Class No. 30956 and another unidentifiable Mogul as they gain the top of the bank on a ballast train viewed from just below Queen Street Bridge. Heavy ballast trains were very much a feature of the bank, some being as much as 400 tons and so requiring considerable assistance. The steam of the rear engine can just be seen emerging from St Davids Tunnel. The track in the foreground was the down line in both senses. The Z will come off in the centre road at Exeter Central and the Mogul alone will work the train forward to at least Exmouth Junction. This looks like a train of chippings rather than ballast and may be on its way to the Southern's Concrete Works just to the east of Blackboy Tunnel.

Opposite bottom - West Country No. 34030 Watersmeet departs from Central with a North Devon Line train, seen drawing forward under the Queen Street Bridge. The engine is at the site of the embarrassing stalling of a steam rail tour in 2006, when the special attempted to come up the bank using the bi-directional line with two engines (76009 and 34067 Tangmere) on the front but nothing on the back. Clearly two on the front is not the same as one on the front and one on the back. With no spare motive power available in Exeter (the nearest being in Plymouth or Westbury) the whole train was allowed to roll back down the hill into St Davids where the passengers alighted to the prospect of finding their own way home.

This page - A quick glance at No. 35023 might suggest wrong-line running, until we see that Merchant Navy Holland Afrika Line has a tail lamp and is backing down to Central from Exmouth Junction. It is seen here entering Blackboy Tunnel on its way to work the up ACE.

Top - *Merchant Navy No. 35009 Shaw Savill lifts the up Atlantic Coast Express from Black Boy Tunnel and over the Exmouth junction as it accelerates into its 3-hour journey to Waterloo. To the east of Exeter Central gradients were much more normal for a mainline being 1 in 100 out of the tunnel and 1 in 400 through the junction.*

Opposite top - *When not working on the bank the Z Class engines were used at Exmouth Junction for shunting. Here No. 30957 is displaying the effectiveness of its design for such work, the slope on the front of the tanks allowing the footplate crew to see the shunter working at the front of the engine. The handle above the buffer beam end provided a degree of security when riding on the front steps. Other duties for these engines included shunting work at Central where, for example, they could be seen inserting restaurant cars into up London trains.*

Opposite bottom - *All that remains of the railway infrastructure in this view from Queen Street Bridge are the bi-directional 'down' line and the up line with the catch siding still in place. The carriage sidings are now a car park and an extension of Exeter College. On the other side the builders' yards are now high-density housing. The view is of the stalled special, 28 March 2006 just short of its destination.*
Picture by Maurice Hopper

Authors comments: It will be noted that in this relatively small collection of pictures there are a number of repeat appearances. This is not surprising in relation to the M7, which is seen twice. Perhaps more surprising is that all the Zs are different members of the Class. It is rather unusual that both 74 Squadron and Watersmeet are also seen twice. The former on two up trains suggesting the pictures were taken over several days. It is known that Philip Conolly visited the area on several occasions. Indeed picture No. 1 - on page 41 in this series is numbered 1278 while No. 5 on page 44 is 3276, suggesting that they were taken in different years. The general impression is of pictures taken in the mid to late fifties, with plenty of red and cream livery and Maunsell coaches to be seen.

BR STANDARD Mk 1 STOCK ON THE SOUTHERN REGION 1951 - 1967: Part 2

Mike King

In part 1, we looked at the original "Royal Wessex" stock and most of the shorter (ie. 3- or 4-coach) sets of permanently-formed vehicles. Now it is time to consider those sets formed of six or more vehicles. These are far more difficult to categorise, as not only were there few identical formations but they tended to change very much more often – not just from year to year depending on the services upon which they were employed, but also from winter to summer depending on traffic levels. Along with this, there was scope for the actual position of each coach to vary within the set and it was not at all uncommon for the formation listed in the Carriage Working Appendices not to be strictly followed out on the line. It all came down to ease of marshalling at such places as Clapham Yard, Eastleigh, Bournemouth West, Rotherhithe Road, etc.: and whether the coach was the correct way round or positioned exactly as the CWN stated was less important than ensuring the correct number of vehicles and ratio of first to third class seats were provided.

As already noted, some of the 3- and 4-coach sets were regularly augmented with other stock (by no means always BR standards) and perhaps the most common augmentation was to cut in two corridor thirds (usually Bulleids) into a set to give a 5 or 6-coach formation – this being especially common on the SW Division at the start of the summer service in June, with the set reverting to original formation once the winter timetable resumed in September. 3-sets 515-19/61-71 were all listed in this form during their first few summers, the further addition of a Maunsell buffet car in the centre making up a 6-coach train. 4-sets 873-6 were similarly made up to between six and eight vehicles during their early years. Some examples are shown in Table 1 (opposite), but despite the long list, by no means every variation has been listed.

Open third S3940, one of 60 such vehicles built at Eastleigh during 1953/4 and allocated to the Southern Region, seen at Folkestone Harbour beach sidings on 17 September 1955, along with other Mk1 thirds and seconds. The open third (later second) was eventually to become the most numerous Mk1 type on the region, with just over 200 examples allocated by 1968, exceeding the number of brake thirds / seconds by about a dozen. Note the roof boards proclaiming 'Continental Express – Short Sea Route' – a reminder that the Channel crossing could be rough and a consideration for many before the days of mass air travel. The beach sidings are now long gone but they provided an interesting shunting manoeuvre at the Harbour station, as access was gained via a chained off crossing half-way along the westernmost platform in a manner unlikely to be acceptable to modern Health and Safety officials. J. H. Aston

Set No	Date	Vehicles	Duty
515	1959-64	35014, 3836, Buffet, 3935, 15914, 35015	Brighton-Plymouth
516	1959-65	35016, 3837, Buffet, 3936, 15902, 35017	Brighton-Plymouth
		In these sets the buffet cars were Maunsell vehicles in 1959-61, Mk1's thereafter.	
517	1959-61	35018, 3830, 15903, Buffet, 3945, 4043, 35019	SW Division
517	1962-64	35018, 3847, 3920, 3830, 15903, Restaurant Car Dining Saloon, 13003, 3945, 4043, 35019	Channel Islands Boat Express
517	1965	34283, 3847, 3920, 3830, Restaurant Car, Dining Saloon, 15903, 15570, 3945, 4043, 34284	Channel Islands Boat Express
		In this the buffet car was a Maunsell in 1959-61, Bulleid or Mk1 vehicles thereafter.	
525	1959-65	34641, 3824, 15567, 15915, 3825, 34642	Waterloo - Exeter
540	1965	34629, 4031, Mk1 Buffet, 4033, 15582, 34630	Brighton - Plymouth
544	11 / 1956	34940, 4040, 15904, S7866S, 15874, 3824, 34941	SE Division
545	11 / 1956	34942, 4037, 15905, S7957S, 15875, 4039, 34943	SE Division
		These two sets were reduced to their listed 3-coach formations from January 1957, once "permanent" long sets 277-9 were ready for traffic (see later).	
548	1964 - 65	34948, 25915, 25910, 16200, 15878, 16201, 4901, 34949	Central & SE Division
551	1964 - 65	34954, 25909, 15881, 25918, 25914, 34955	Oxted Line
558	1963 - 64	34968, 4008, 15888, 1757, 15000, 4014, 34969	Portsmouth - Cardiff
560	1962 - 63	35012, 15913, S7633S, 9, S7887S, 4385, 35013	SW Division
561	1963	34970, 15889, 1720, 34971	Waterloo - Lymington
866	1962 - 63	34233, 24302, 1850, 15024, 34234	Brighton - Cardiff
867	1962 - 63	34235, 24303, Mk1 Minibuffet, 15025, 34236	Brighton - Cardiff
873	1955 - 58	34247, 24308, 15030, S5892S, 15031, S91S, 24309, 34248	SE Division
873	1959 - 61	34247, 24308, 15030, S5892S, 15031, S91S, S1864S, 24309, 34248	SE Division
873	1961 - 62	34247, 24308, S91S, 15030, 15031, S105S, 24309, 34248	Central Division
874	1953 - 61	34249, 24310, S51S, 15032, S5903S, S52S, S53S, 34250	SE Division
874	1963 - 64	34249, 24310, 15032, Buffet, Dining Saloon, S5903S, 34250 (Bulleid or Mk1 catering vehicles)	Southampton Boat
875	1953 - 61	34251, 24311, S84S, 15033, S5899S, S88S, S89S, 34252	SE Division
876	1953 - 62	34253, 24312, S7631S, 15034, S54S, 34254	Oxted Line
880		This set changed formation every year between 1952 and 1965, being a basic 9-set including a Maunsell or Mk1 buffet car!	Bournemouth-York / Newcastle
881	1962	34263, 24317, 1852, 15039, 34264	Brighton - Bournemouth
885	1964	34271, 15043, 1019, 1716, 4041, 34272	Waterloo - Bournemouth
887	1960	34275, 15045, 1852, 24323, 34276	SW Division
888	1960 - 61	34277, 24324, 1851, 15046, 34278	Brighton - Bournemouth
889	1956 - 61	34279, 24325, 15047, 15901, 3916, 34280	Portsmouth - Cardiff
889	1962 - 64	34279, 24325, 15047, 1852, 15901, 3916, 34280	Portsmouth - Cardiff
891	1960 - 61	34283, 24327, 1850, 15049, 34284	Brighton - Cardiff

Perhaps the first ordinary longer sets to be permanently formed from new stock were numbers 277-79, which arrived on the SE Division in late 1956. At first their intended duties were covered by augmenting 3-sets 544 and 545 – maybe their arrival was delayed - as listed above but from January 1957 they commenced service, formed as shown in Table 2, (probably including the two Maunsell buffet cars from sets 544/45).

TABLE 2			
Set No	**Date**	**Vehicles**	**Duty**
277	1957 - 61	35004, 4374, 4373, Buffet, 15907, 15906, 35005	SE Division
277	1962 - 63	35004, S1442S, 4374, 4373, 15907, Mk 1 Buffet, 15906, 4018, 3944, 35005	Waterloo - Weymouth
277	1964	35004, 15906, 35005 only	SW Division
278	1957 - 61	35006, 4376, 4375, Buffet, 15909, 15908, 35007	SE Division
278	1962 - 64	35006, S1493S, 4376, 4375, 15909, Mk1 Buffet, 15908, 4025, 3943, 35007	Waterloo - Weymouth
278	1965	As in 1964 less S1493S	SW Division
279	1957	35008, 4378, 4377, Buffet, 15911, 15910, 35009	SE Division
		Nos. 35008, 4377/8 were all destroyed at St Johns (Lewisham) on 4 December 1957	
279	1958 - 61	34631, 4380, 4379, Buffet, 15911, 15910, 35009	SE Division
279	1962 - 64	34631, 4005, 4007, 4379, 4380, 3506, 3507, 35009	Newhaven Night Boat
279	1965	34277, 4007, 4379, 3506, 3507, 4380, 35009	Newhaven Night Boat

One of the 15 open seconds built specifically for continental boat train service in 1953 and so labelled on the doors; S3506 is seen at the same location as S3940, in company with S3505 and a 12-wheeled Pullman, illustrating somewhat the varied composition of SE Division boat trains. In fact this set was remarkably tidily formed on that day, as it included three Mk1 open thirds and three open seconds, either side of the Pullman car. However, the brake end coaches were a SECR 'Continental' and a Maunsell restriction 1 unclassed open saloon, so variety was being maintained!

J. H. Aston

Several other long sets also appeared on the region at various times but rather than being formed from new vehicles these were drawn from a mixture of existing loose coaches and transfers from other regions. As time went on, this was to become more common as the Mk1 programme began to draw to a close in 1963/4. Examples are shown in Table 3.

Set No	Date	Vehicles	Duty
		TABLE 3	
237	1961 on	Included open seconds 3926-31 with Bulleid brakes and a corridor first – formation changed regularly	Central Division Special traffic
237	1963	S3949S, 3926, 3927, 3932, S7640S, 3929, 3930, 3931, S3961S	Central Division Special traffic
280	1960 - 61	34956, 15882, 15000, Buffet, 4005, 4007, 34957	Central Division
280	1962	34956, 15882, 15000, 34957	Waterloo - Weymouth
280	1963 - 65	34956, 15882, 34957 only	SW Division
427	1957 - 61	34992, S7625S, Buffet, 3832, 3833, 34993	SW Division
		In 1961 the buffet was brand new Kitchen/Buffet car 1553	
427	1962 - 63	34992, 15910, 34993 only	SW Division
427	1964 - 65	34835, 25906, 13143, 16205, 25907, 34925	SW Division
468	1961 on	Included Mk1 open seconds with Bulleid brakes and a first – formation changed regularly	SE Division Special traffic
468	1961	S3958S, 3940, 3939, 3938, 3937, 3070, 3934, 3933, 3932, S3959S	SE Division Special traffic
468	1962	S3958S, 3940, 3939, 3938, 3937, 3934, 3933, 3925, 15911, S7644S, S3959S + vans	Newhaven Day Boat
468	1963 - 64	S3958S, 3940, 3939, 3938, 3937, Mk1 Buffet, 3934, 3933, 15911, S7644S, S3959S + vans	Newhaven Day Boat
468	1965	S3958S, 3939, First, Mk1 Buffet, 15911, 3934, S3959S	Newhaven Day Boat
		Note the declining popularity of the Newhaven boat services (seen also with set 279)	
766	1964 - 65	34790, 25913, 25912, 16204, 15581, 4905, 34934	Oxted Line
		Five of these were ex-Western Region in maroon livery and stayed in that colour	
985	1964 - 65	34940, 25916, 25917, 16221, 16220, 25924, 25944, 34951	Oxted Line
		Six of these were also ex-Western Region and may also have retained maroon.	

BR Diagram 24 was the most numerous Mk1 catering vehicle on the region, with up to 29 allocated from 1960 onwards. This is the 'buffet' side of S1718, labelled 'Buffet Restaurant Car' and formed in an up West of England express at Seaton Junction in the early 1960s. This was one of the BRCW-built vehicles on BR2 bogies. Dining facilities are provided by the adjacent Bulleid open second. This coach later became 4-REP buffet 69323, withdrawn for electric stock conversion in March 1967.

Author's collection

The following sets were formed in 1965 from Bullied brakes and Mk1 vehicles, set 66 being a former Bulleid 2-set augmented with a Bulleid composite to four vehicles. Note that the firsts were new Mk2 vehicles and that each set had a brake vehicle nearer the centre, to assist at station stops with short platforms, now that most Exeter trains were calling at all stations beyond Salisbury.

Table 4			
Set No	**Date**	**Vehicles**	**Duty**
66	1965	S4374S, S5916S, Mk1 Minibuffet, S6703S	Waterloo - Exeter
701	1965	S4371S, Mk 1 Buffet, Mk1 Dining Saloon, 13392, 34646, 15898, 24322, S4381S	Waterloo - Exeter
702	1965	S4376S, Mk1 Buffet, Mk1 Dining Saloon, 13393, 34645, 15565, 24318, S4377S	Waterloo - Exeter
703	1965	S4378S, Mk1 Buffet, Mk1 Open Second, 13394, 15568, S4380S, 24307	Waterloo - Exeter

Opposite top - The 'corridor' side of S1760 at Bournemouth Central on 31 August 1962, formed in an up express for Waterloo. This had been built earlier in that year by The Pressed Steel Co. and ran on 'Commonwealth' bogies. By this date the new Mk1 catering vehicles were replacing the Bulleid vehicles on many trains, allowing these to be used as relief cars and the ageing Maunsell vehicles to be withdrawn.

AE. West R4023

Opposite bottom - Just two Diagram 25 kitchen / buffet cars were allocated to the Southern Region. This is S1552 at Exeter Central on 8 September 1962, coupled between a Bulleid composite (left) and Maunsell open second S1429S (right), the latter providing dining facilities. All await attachment to the next London-bound train. Note that no side buffers appear to be fitted and that the kitchen compartment door droplights are painted green. BR2 bogies are provided.

A E. West R4062

This page - Hardly a Mk1 vehicle, but formed in Southampton boat set 352 at Clapham Yard in 1958, between Bulleid first S7619S and a Mk1 open second, probably S3842. Green Pullman buffet car No. 184 was formerly Hastings line Pullman 'Theodora' until July 1958 and would be renumbered as BR S7874S in November 1960. It is now preserved in Pullman umber and cream on the Kent & East Sussex Railway. There were seven green Pullmans between 1958 and 1963 – six were the former Hastings line cars, the seventh was formerly 'The Hadrian Bar' and they were most often used on Southampton boat trains.

R. Lacy, HMRS Collection

Loose Stock

In a sense, the coaches allocated to the 'Royal Wessex' could have been termed loose vehicles in that they were not formed into a numbered set, but being specifically dedicated for that service they have not been considered as such. The largest group of nominally loose coaches were the open thirds (seconds from June 1956) delivered from Eastleigh and Swindon between 1953 and 1957. A total of 132 were allocated new to the Southern

Region during this period and several were immediately placed in Southampton boat sets 350-54, replacing various Bulleid coaches, but initially the sets retained their Maunsell composite brakes at each end. It was not until 1956/7 that more Mk1 brake seconds were delivered and from then on the sets assumed more of a 'Mk1' look, with just a Bulleid first and / or composite included. Catering vehicles would be 'cut into' the sets as required. Examples are shown in Table 5:

Table 5		
Set No	**Date**	**Vehicles**
350	1956 - 58	34994, 3828, 3829, S7617S, 3915, 3831, 3836, 34995
350	1963	34994, 3828, 3829, S7617S, S5809S, 3831, 3840, 34995
351	1956 - 58	34996, 3837, 3838, S7627S, 3839, 3834, 3835, 34997
351	1963	34996, 3839, 3838, S7627S, S5810S, 3834, 3835, 34997
352	1956 - 58	34998, 3840, 3841, S7619S, 3842, 3843, 3844, 34999
352	1959 - 63	34998, 3842, 3841, S7619S, S5811S, 3843, 3844, 34999
353	1957 - 62	35000, S7608S, S7609S, S7618S, 3847, 3848, 3849, 35001
353	1963	35000, S7609S, S7618S, S7610S, 3065, Buffet, 3848, 3849, 35001
353	1964	As in 1963, less Buffet (Mk1 or Pullman vehicle)
354	1957 - 62	35002, S7621S, S7620S, S7615S, 3917, 3918, 3919, 35003
354	1963	35002, S7621S, S7620S, S7623S, 3064, Buffet, 3918, 3919, 35003
354	1964	As in 1963, less Buffet (Mk1 or Pullman vehicle)

BR STANDARD Mk 1 STOCK ON THE SOUTHERN REGION 1951 - 1967: Part 2

The Pullman buffet cars could have been from the seven "green" Pullmans in BR service between 1958 and 1963 or those in the more usual umber and cream livery. Note also that sets 353/54 catered for a higher proportion of first class passengers as might be expected on boat trains of that era, but it was not unusual for a "scratch" set to be formed entirely of first class coaches, for which Mk1 open firsts 3063-70 could be used, marshalled between two of the six brake firsts (two Maunsells and four "Ironclads") that were normally kept at Clapham Yard or Southampton New Docks for the purpose.

The South Eastern and Newhaven boat sets were far less tidy in appearance than the equivalent Southampton boat trains during the 1950s and these (numbered on paper as Boat Sets 1-10 but not marked on the vehicles themselves) usually included two Mk1 open thirds and two dedicated Mk1 open seconds from 1953 onwards, together with a former SECR "Continental" brake first at the London end, a Maunsell nondescript brake at the other with a selection of other "Continentals", "Ironclads", Maunsells, Bulleids and maybe a couple of Pullmans within the 11/12 coaches thrown in for good measure, plus a couple of "utility" vans for luggage. The dedicated open seconds were a unique batch of 15 vehicles (Nos. 3500-14) specially constructed for continental boat trains - to match the three-class system in operation across Europe - but this ceased in June 1956 upon the abolition of second class and, having lost their *raison d'être*, these coaches were then demoted to open thirds; now, of course, described as second – all very confusing! However, their 2+1 seating meant that they seated 16 less passengers than a standard open third (second), which caused rostering and seat reservation problems, so they were upgraded to first class in 1959. They still failed to find much employment and nos. 3501/10 became first class dining saloons before being transferred to the Eastern Region, together with 3504/12-14 in 1968. A few entered SR departmental service but as a class they were some of the earliest Mk1 withdrawals and all had gone by 1970.

Few true corridor firsts were allocated to the region before 1964 – no. 13143 arrived from the Western Region in 1963 (placed in set 427) – but in August-November 1964 a batch of 20 Mk2 integrally-constructed corridor firsts arrived, in green with yellow cantrail stripes and these were soon appropriated for Southampton boat trains, the "Golden Arrow" and the "Night Ferry". Truly this was the shape of things to come, but it would be many years before Mk2 vehicles became a common sight on the region. Other corridor firsts were transferred in 1965/6, but with the intention of converting them to 4-REP/TC electric vehicles rather than augmenting the existing steam-hauled stock. Some more open seconds were received at the same time, for the same intended purpose whilst some already SR-allocated seconds, composites and buffet cars were taken for conversion from mid-1966 onwards. By no means all of the electric stock transfers actually saw much service during their short stay as locomotive-hauled stock. To compensate for the loss of open seconds from elsewhere, the Southern released a number of Bulleid open seconds for the Eastern and Scottish Regions and some of these were actually the final Bulleid corridors to remain in service, the last being withdrawn in 1970; two years later than any remaining SR-allocated vehicles.

A batch of brake composites arrived in early 1964 – amongst the last new Mk1 construction for the Southern Region and several of these ran as loose vehicles on Waterloo-West of England through services until these ceased in September of that year but others were incorporated into Bulleid Bournemouth line 6-coach sets in the 290-300 series – sets 298/300 having one at each end while 296 included no less than three, along with other Mk1 stock, giving it a most curious formation. Details of these are shown in Table 6, by which time the Bulleid restaurant cars and other coaches in these sets were also being replaced by Mk1 catering vehicles, to be described on the next page.

Table 6		
Set No	**Date**	**Vehicles**
296	1964	21267, 4000, 21270, Mk1 Open Second, MK1 Buffet, 21271
298	1965	21269, S1459S, S5748S, Mk1 Buffet, 3921, 21268
299	1965	21266, S7648S, Mk1 Buffet, 3941, S4368S
300	1965	21272, S1481S, S5750S, Mk1 Buffet, 3833, 21273
Set 290 also deserves mention here as this included Mk1 open first 3067 in 1960, later former "Wessex" restaurant first No. 9 for a time, as follows: -		
290	6 / 1960	S4349S, S5740S, S7677S, 3067, S7881S, S1451S, S4350S
290	1960 - 61	S4349S, S5740S, S7677S, 9 , S7881S, S1451S, S4350S

Opposite - The train now standing on platform 3!! Mk1 full brake M80753 was derailed at Vauxhall late in the afternoon of 6 May 1958, causing complete chaos for the evening rush hour. Passengers seldom used the fast line platforms at Vauxhall so this was a convenient place to lift the vehicle out of the way pending later removal. This was the scene two days after the derailment. The van is in crimson lake and cream; SR-allocated green BG's would not appear for another seven years, numbered S80561/94/695/875/93/926/33/45/49, 81039/50/153/273/289/292/345/510/542.

J. H. Aston

Once 3-sets numbered between 541 and 550 were re-formed in 1964, odd loose brake seconds could be seen – prior to this they were a very rare sight. Similarly loose composites were confined to prototype coach 15000 and orthodox coach 15915 at times during the 1950s and it was not until 1964 that others could be seen. Even loose corridor seconds were uncommon until 4-sets 866-91 had yielded theirs up in 1962 and only the open thirds/seconds were at all numerous. Some more corridor seconds and composites were acquired from the Western Region in 1963; most being dual-heated were used on the Central and SE Divisions. Any of these loose coaches could turn up as strengthening vehicles on any service during the 'set' era, but after about March 1966, when permanently formed sets were abandoned until the end of steam in July 1967, any combination was possible. One wonders how the staff coped with this sudden change in procedure after years of being instructed always to maintain the stock in fixed set formations? The carriage working notices suddenly went from publishing a list of set formations and their intended workings just to a numerical list of coach numbers. It certainly did not make for tidy looking train formations. Cynics said it was to make the new electric services look even better…

Once full electrified services commenced in July 1967, new set formations were again detailed in the CWNs, but the whole process was never pursued with the same vigour as before and many of the published formations existed only on paper and not in fact.

Catering vehicles

For almost ten years the only Mk1 catering vehicles on the region had been the 'Wessex' triple of 9/80009/1006. The provision of such extensive catering was seldom required on the Southern – few journeys could accommodate the double sittings required to maintain economical use of all three coaches. Coupled with this was the general move away from full meals to the provision of lighter snacks, so it is hardly surprising that the three were split up and by 1960 both diners were in use separately – No. 9 on Bournemouth services in conjunction with a Bulleid buffet car and 1006 on the "Night Ferry". Kitchen car 80009 was afforded the luxury of a repaint in green by 1960 but seems to have languished at Clapham yard for most of its time until withdrawn four years later.

From 1960 new Mk1 buffet cars (of two types) began to appear on the region – a total of 31 plus five mini-buffets eventually being allocated. The single diner third (now second) to BR Diagram 56, coach 1006, was augmented by five more between 1962 and 1964 – three being identical cars 1007/10/13 and two others to Diagram 61 (nos. 1018/19) and these were structurally identical to the open seconds – but with loose seating, fixed tables to each seating bay and unclassed. The five mini-buffets were for use on routes requiring only minimal catering facilities such as Brighton-Bournemouth and Cardiff trains. It made sense to maximise the use of these new, modern vehicles and from 1962 the new cars progressively replaced the Bulleid buffets in Bournemouth line 6-coach sets 290-300. Permanent allocations were not made and coaches moved around as necessary – the usual arrangement followed in the past with all SR catering stock except in these 6-coach sets. (Table 7)

During the period under review, the Southern had four cafeteria cars allocated as well – reinforcing the "light snack"-catering ethos. Two of these were Maunsell conversions but the others were a pair of Gresley LNER rebuilds (numbers S9211E and S9213E) and these were running in green livery from 1955 until 1963. Just to add a little more variation, in 1966 five more LNER buffet cars arrived (nos. 9117/19/25/27/34) but these retained their E prefix and suffix letters and maroon livery, although it is believed one may have been repainted blue and grey before withdrawal. What was it that was said about variety at the beginning of Part 1?

Of course, Mk1 coaches from other regions were a regular sight on the Southern as well as those allocated, but this would not have been so apparent in the crimson lake and cream era. Once the Southern returned to green for its own stock and the other regions adopted maroon then they became more obvious and some of the more unusual types could also be seen – even including the 1957 prototypes – the author has a picture of one of the 1957 open firsts, taken at Southampton Central in 1958 – so in reality and with modellers in mind, the final comment must be that anything was possible. At the end of this article will be found a complete list of all Mk1 stock allocated from new to the Southern Region, together with some notes on later transfers, although this last cannot be claimed to be exhaustive without becoming endless as few consecutively-numbered batches of vehicles were received.

Non-Passenger Coaching Stock

These are the last group of vehicles to be dealt with. Perhaps because the Southern Region had getting on for two

Table 7
Set 291 included buffet 1762 in 1962, 1723 a year later.
Set 292 included buffet 1760 in 1962/3.
Set 293 included buffet 1723 in 1962, 1717 a year later.
Set 294 included buffet 1763 in 1964.
Set 295 included buffet 1719 in 1962.
Set 297 included buffet 1764 in 1963.
Set 299 included buffet 1719 in 1963.
Set 300 included buffet 1717 in 1964 and doubtless there were many other changes.

thousand of its own "utility" vans, it took until 1958 before any equivalent Mk1 stock was allocated and even by 1972 this amounted to just four types. The allocation of such stock is a much more arbitrary matter than passenger coaches, since by the nature of the traffic dealt with, the vehicles were likely to wander the length and breadth of the country - just look at how often SR utility vans could be seen many miles away from SR metals. Conversely, vehicles from elsewhere were a daily sight on the Southern Region after 1951, so the fact that such Mk1 stock had W, E or M prefixes was probably unimportant. None appear to have ever been allocated to the Scottish Region, unlike the passenger carrying vehicles.

The BR standard full brake (coded BG) first appeared in 1951 and was the only corridor vehicle built on the shorter (56ft 11in) underframe – 58ft over body. No doubt this was done to increase route availability, but this did not extend to the Tonbridge-Hastings line and the only Mk1s to be permitted here were the 4w and bogie GUV/CCT's, to be described next. Most of the full brakes built up to 1957 were painted crimson lake and cream, but two batches (Nos. 80617-71 and 80965-81014, built in 1954 and 1956 respectively) were given unlined crimson. From 1957 lined maroon became general and a few received WR prestige chocolate and cream. Two of these vans (W80713/14 and they retained their W prefixes) were appropriated by the Southern Region for use on the "Bournemouth Belle" from about 1962 and certainly matched the Pullmans far better than the blood and custard or maroon vehicle previously employed. Both were replaced, firstly by green examples in late 1965 and then by blue and grey vans in mid-1966 (some of the first repaints to this colour scheme) and these again failed to harmonise well with the Pullmans. It was not until 1965 that any full brakes were allocated to the Southern Region, when 18 transfers from the LMR arrived just in time to be painted green – possibly the last repaints in this colour.

The next new arrivals were the bogie covered carriage trucks/general utility vans, 130 of which were delivered in 1959. These were 57ft long and had flat sides with end doors, vaguely resembling a much shorter LMS design. Interestingly, the Southern had 120 gangwayed bogie luggage vans and 10 older scenery vans in service until 1957-59 and perhaps these were seen as direct replacements. All were finished in lined maroon livery, being repainted green at first overhaul – which seemed to occur more quickly than might have been expected! Eight were used on the Surbiton-Okehampton car carrier train, which ran for five summers from 1960, but otherwise these vehicles were much in use on parcels and van trains. The equivalent 4-wheeled CCT, similar in construction and 37ft long, was introduced in 1959 but although a common sight on the region, none were given green livery or S prefixes during the steam era. Some were SR allocated later, but by then were running in rail blue livery. Both types had a prototype vehicle, which differed considerably from the production batches. This is relevant as far as the Southern Region is concerned, because 34 similar ferry vans were constructed (four bogies and 30 4-wheelers) between 1955 and 1961 specifically for continental services. Strictly speaking these were not classed as passenger vehicles at all and were painted freight stock bauxite and numbered in the wagon series in order to reinforce this. However, as vacuum-fitted vehicles they could be seen as tail traffic on passenger trains and in van trains, mostly on the SE Division.

The final design of Mk1 non-passenger vehicle was the horsebox. This was 27ft 6in long and featured a distinct curved body profile – again to improve route availability but still not Tonbridge-Hastings. A total of 115 were completed in 1958/9 and 56 were allocated to the Southern and given green livery. Their arrival allowed the withdrawal of the last LSWR and LBSCR horseboxes but soon after horse traffic deserted the railways and all were withdrawn by 1971 after a lifetime of comparative disuse.

No Mk1 travelling post office vans were SR-allocated until 1974, when just six were received for the Waterloo-Dorchester / Weymouth service, replacing the then-ageing Maunsell vans still employed at that time, but that belongs firmly to the 'rail blue' era.

A total of 130 bogie general utility vans were SR-allocated from 1959. This is S86796 at Clapham Yard on 6 August 1959, in as-delivered lined maroon livery. Note how the waist lining fails to recommence to the right of the lettering block. It was not very long before many of them were repainted unlined green. The solitary GUV prototype, W86500, differed from all the production examples by omitting the centre pair of doors.

D Cullum 3485, courtesy The Lens of Sutton Association

Running Numbers	BR Diagram	Vehicle Type	Construction Date or Transfer	Remarks
		Summary of BR Mk1 Vehicles Allocated to the Southern Region, 1951-67		
9	36	Dining 1st	York 1951	'Royal Wessex' stock
1006	56	Dining 3rd	York 1951	'Royal Wessex' stock
1007 / 10 / 13	56	Dining 2nd	Ex-WR in 1962	Seating now unclassed
1018 / 19	61	Dining 2nd	EX-NER in 1963 / 4	Seating now unclassed
1552 / 53	25	Kitchen / Buffet	Cravens 1961	BR2 bogies
1714 / 15	24	Buffet / Restaurant	Ex-ER in 1965 / 6	BR2 bogies
1716 - 24	24	Buffet / Restaurant	BRCW 1960	BR2 bogies
1755 - 72	24	Buffet / Restaurant	Pressed Steel 1962	Commonwealth bogies
1849 - 52	98	Minibuffet	Wolverton 1960	BR1 bogies
1881	99	Minibuffet	Wolverton 1962	Commonwealth bogies
3063 - 70	73	Open 1st	Doncaster 1955	Mostly on boat trains
3500 - 14	90	Open 2nd (boat train)	Eastleigh 1953	To ordinary 2nd 1956, then to open 1st 1959
3701	92	Open 2nd	Ex-WR in 1967	Former prototype coach
3824 - 49	93	Open 3rd	Eastleigh 1953 / 4	Open 2nd from June 1956
3913 - 46	93	Open 3rd	Eastleigh 1954	Open 2nd from June 1956
3998 - 4047	93	Open 3rd	Swindon 1956	Open 2nd from June 1956
4373 - 94	93	Open 2nd	Swindon 1957	
In range 3738 - 4560	93	Open 2nd	Ex-WR, ER & ScR between 1963 - 67	Many for electric stock conversions - 45 coaches
4900 - 16 & 5024	89	Open 2nd	Ex-WR in 1963	Most duel heated
13003	116	Corridor 1st	Swindon 1951	'Royal Wessex' stock
13143	116	Corridor 1st	Ex-WR in 1963	Dual heated
In range 13000 to 13179	116	Corridor 1st	Ex-WR, LMR & ER in 1965 / 66	Most for electric stock conversions - 42 coaches
13387 - 13406	120	Corridor 1st	Derby 1964	MkII stock - the first to be SR allocated
15000	127	Corridor Compo.	Eastleigh 1950	Prototype Mk1 coach
15021 - 23	128	Corridor Compo.	Eastleigh 1951	'Royal Wessex' stock

Opposite top - *One of the four Mk1 bogie ferry vans, B889203, as outshopped in 1958 without droplights or side windows – originally these were provided as per the general utility vans. Like the prototype GUV, no centre pairs of doors were provided. Freight stock bauxite livery is carried, together with the inscription 'Southern Region Ferry Van' along the centre of the sides. Beyond is another van of the same type. BR freight stock Diagram 292 describes the vehicle as a 14 Ton Scenery Van for Continental Ferry Service.*

Author's collection

Opposite bottom - *The equivalent 4-wheeled ferry van design – B889002 as built in 1958 complete with side windows and a door droplight, identical to prototype covered carriage truck E94100 and measuring 30ft 9in long over body. BR freight stock Diagram 291 describes them as 14 Ton Motor Car Vans for Continental Ferry Service.*

Author's collection

Running Numbers	BR Diagram	Vehicle Type	Construction Date or Transfer	Remarks
15024 - 49	128	Corridor Compo.	Eastleigh 1951 / 52	For 4-coach sets
15563 - 82	128	Corridor Compo.	Met. Camm. 1955	For 3-coach sets
15871 - 15915	128	Corridor Compo.	Met. Camm. 1956	For 3-coach sets & sets 277 - 79
15425 & between 16198 - 221	128	Corridor Compo.	Ex-WR in 1963	Dual heated - 11 coaches
21251	172	Brake Compo.	Swindon 1962	Possibly ex-WR in 1965
21263 - 75	172	Brake Compo.	Derby 1964	Dual heated
24169	147	Corridor 3rd	Derby 1951	'Royal Wessex' stock
24302 - 27	147	Corridor 3rd	Eastleigh 1952	For 4-coach sets
24980 / 81	146	Corridor 2nd	Ex-ER in 1967	Later dual heated
In range 25906 - 25972	147	Corridor 2nd.	Ex-WR in 1963 - 5	Dual heat - 21 coaches
34155 - 59	182	Brake 3rd	Wolverton 1951	'Royal Wessex' stock
34233 - 84	182	Brake 3rd	Eastleigh 1951/52	For 4-coach sets
34613 - 30	182	Brake 3rd	Gloucester 1955	For 3-coach sets
34631 - 54	182	Brake 3rd	Charles Roberts 1954/55	For 3-coach sets
34934 - 35023	182	Brake 2nd	Met. Camm. 1956/57	For 3-coach sets, boat sets & sets 277-279
34790 / 835 & 34925	182	Brake 2nd	Ex-WR in 1963	Dual heated - 3 coaches
41060 - 64	312	N/Corr Compo.	Swindon 1956	For Exmouth branch
43374 - 83	372	N/Corr Brake 3rd	Swindon 1956	For Exmouth branch
46280 - 98	327	N/Corr 3rd	Swindon 1956	For Exmouth branch
In range 46005 - 46275	327	N/Corr 2nd	Ex-WR in 1964	For Waterloo - Basingstoke services
80009	700	Kitchen Car	Doncaster 1951	'Royal Wessex' stock
Between 80561 - 81542	711	Full brake	Ex-LMR in 1965	18 vehicles, repainted in green livery
86705 - 834	811	Gen. Utility Van	Pressed Steel 1959	Lined maroon livery
Between 94104 - 94920	816	4w-covered Carriage Truck	Ex-WR, LMR & ER, post 1967	Rail blue livery - at least 136 vehicles
96359 - 414	751	4w - Horsebox	Earlestown 1958	Green livery
B889000 - 29	291	4w - Ferry Van	Lancing 1958 / 61	Freight stock (bauxite)
B889200 - 3	292	Bogie Ferry Van	Eastleigh 1955	Freight stock (bauxite)

Source: Complete listing of BR standard Mk1 vehicles allocated to the Southern Region, taken from Waterloo Carriage Stock Register, loaned to the author by Denis Cullum in 1979.

Opposite top - *Ferry van B889010 as running in 1964 with all windows sheeted in, which is how all 30 vans ended their days, in the early 1980s. Note the electric cable connections below the buffers. Westinghouse brakes were provided to enable the ferry vans to continue their journey beyond Dunkirk. How often they did so is unknown.* Author's collection

Opposite bottom - *The BR horseboxes were destined for a life of virtual disuse, certainly for the purpose for which they were built. S96410 stands condemned in the rain at Micheldever sidings about 1969, surrounded by others of the same type. The other side is a mirror image save for the toilet window being opaque and having a ventilator in the toplight. Some vans carried their running number in the narrow panel over the near pair of doors, allowing easy identification when the doors were open. Most maroon examples were allocated to the Eastern Region, with just four to the WR and five to the LMR, giving some indication of where most racehorse traffic originated. A few were used by Bertram Mills Circus' train.* The Lens of Sutton Association

Above - Still in wartime unlined black with SOUTHERN on the tank side, No. 2008 is at the buffer stops in the goods yard. Behind the façade of Olby's local builders' merchants is prominent. Above the large sign a vestige of the recent war remains – 'Dig for Victory' the sign exclaims – in austerity Britain 'Digging for Peace' might be more appropriate: to improve the rationed diet of the times. The Southdown coach is interesting, GUF 742, one of the first batch of 25 post war Leyland Tiger PS1/1, numbered 1242 in the Southdown fleet. According to 'The Classic Buses' website little is known of its history – still active in 1956 it was gone by 1961. The vehicle was a 31 seat coach with body from Eastern Coachworks.

Left - No. 2008 shows the classic Marsh 4-4-2 tank lines – when re-built the opportunity to fit a 'River' tank-like cab helped the locos conform to the composite loading gauge and widened their availability. Unlike the express and highly successful I3 tanks with their superheated boilers and 6' 9" driving wheels, the I1X's were a more mixed traffic design with 5' 6" driving wheels and saturated boilers. The livery looks pretty care worn and she never received a 30000 series number or BR emblem.

I1X TANKS (and memories) at BOGNOR REGIS

Bill Allen

Bognor Regis 'MPD' was, post–war, a sub-shed of Horsham (75D). Electrification had diminished the importance of the depot, which, pre-war, had allocations of Brighton Atlantics & B4s for the principal trains to London, Stroudley D tanks for local services and sundry other tanks, including E4 and E1 types for local freight etc. The depot, however, still had a role post war as a signing on point for enginemen, as well as servicing and turning for the local rosters on goods and parcels that were still steam hauled. Weekends in the summer also brought an influx of excursion trains, some steam hauled that needed servicing before returning in the evening. And in the immediate years of the 1940s and 50s, the depot and adjoining yards were used as a storage point for locomotives either not required or, in some cases, pre-withdrawal. The photographs accompanying illustrate this latter aspect of Bognor's post war history.

The I1X class were rebuilds of the spectacularly unsuccessful Marsh I1 tanks. Boilers surplus to requirements when a number of B4 4-4-0s were rebuilt by Robert Billington into the B4X type, were used to create the I1X class, which became a much more useful locomotive seen on the many steam lines around Brighton, Tunbridge Wells and Eastbourne. After nationalisation Brighton works produced examples of Fairburn 2-6-4 tanks that then took over the duties of the well established I3 tanks. In turn and on the cascading down principle, the I3s took over the I1X roles which left the I1Xs with little work on only a few local duties around Eastbourne. Consequently the rest of the class were placed in store with only occasional forays when locos were needed – Christmas parcels in 1948 / 49 / 50 being an example. The last survivor to be withdrawn was 32002 in July 1951. D.L.Bradley in 'Locomotives of the LBSCR - Part 3' is a useful source history of the class and his concluding sentence reads , "During 1950 several of the class, including No 2002 were in store at Bognor in company with the unfinished 'Leaders' 36002/3. All built at Brighton works". The Xpress Loco register 'Volume 1 (SR 1949 – 61)' gives allocations of SR locos during the period of the 1950s. Nos. 32008 and 32596 are listed at Bognor Regis from May 1949 – April 1950 and No. 32002 in April 1950. All had departed by September 1950, No. 32002 to Three Bridges (75E) and Nos. 32008 and 32596 to New Cross.

My father's photographs depict two I1Xs at the rear of the goods yard – one is clearly No. 32008 but the identity of the second cannot be determined. Sadly he didn't choose to photograph the 'Leaders' – but photos do exist of Nos. 36002/3 in Bognor shed and have been published in Kevin Robertson's books on the Leader story. The modern, controversial and ultimately unsuccessful Leader was designed by Bulleid to be capable of the very duties that the earlier Marsh tanks had undertaken. It was doubly ironic that both classes of locomotive were stored together – out of use and, in the Leader's case out of mind, in Bognor.

The third photograph was taken a little earlier and again features a loco in store in the yard at the back of Bognor shed. It depicts the author aged between 3 and 4 late in 1946. Four B4Xs had been allocated to Horsham in 1946 (Nos. 2045 / 50 / 55 / 67), but as D.L.Bradley reported "...they were not required and were stored in the open at Bognor. They were steamed again for Christmas traffic that year". By 1949 Nos. 2045 / 50 & 67 were at Bricklayers Arms – no doubt stored at New Cross and No. 2055 at Eastbourne again probably stored in the remains of Eastbourne shed. All were withdrawn in 1951.

Clearly it is winter as I have a winter coat on! The B4X is on a siding next to the coaling stack and in the background the two road shed can be seen with locos in steam. The shed was demolished in 1956 leaving one wall and some office accommodation. The just visible water tank also survived until final closure. Billington's rebuilds of the B4 class produced a loco which lacked the inspiration of the Maunsell rebuilds of Wainwright D and E. While modernised, the front end remained original and this lack of efficiency and capacity to use steam to the maximum meant they never rose to achieve the exploits of the D1 and E1 classes. They took their turn on the expresses of the Central section of the Southern Railway pre–war, but electrification ended their top link careers and their final days were on more mundane tasks.

Left - *The fourth photograph was taken at the same time as that on the previous page and shows both Father and Son. We are posed between the B4X and a C2X: which would have been on the daily goods, a Three Bridges (75E) duty. The C2X is difficult to identify but may be 2536. In the background the goods yard can be seen.*

Bottom - *No. s21C149 Anti-Aircraft Command leaving Bognor Regis light engine in the Spring of 1948. As yet un-named but with a cover concealing the name plate (or space where it would appear). Locomotives running in after a visit to the Works sometimes came to Bognor shed to turn on the table before returning to Brighton. From Richard Derry's 'The Book of the West Country and Battle of Britain Pacifics' we know this engine was on works from 1/2/48 to 13/3/48. At that time it was re-numbered with an 's' prefix to the number and British Railways on the tender but retained the attractive Malachite Green livery with horizontal stripes. The naming ceremony was at Waterloo on 28 April 1948 so this dates the photograph fairly accurately. No. 34049 was always allocated to the SW Division at Salisbury, Nine Elms and Exmouth Junction. Never re-built and withdrawn in December 1963, it was cut up at Eastleigh in June 1964.*

Top - *In early BR / late SR days No. C39, a Bulleid Q1, leaves Bognor on a goods train. The locomotive is about to cross the level crossing over the main road into the town. On the left is the Richmond Arms Public House and the SR sign indicates the walk to the station. On summer week-ends this bottleneck was a continuous traffic jam even in those relatively low density car ownership days. Buses, coaches, cars and cycles queued as trains left and ar-rived at the station. All the service trains were EMUs as the line had been electrified in 1938. 4-CORs & 4-BUFs on the fasts; 2-BILs, 2-HALs and 2 NOLs on the semi-fasts and locals. But in this electrified world the goods, parcels, fish trains and in summer some excursion trains were steam.*

Bottom - *The afternoon goods leaves Bognor viewed from the footbridge that crossed the line by the level crossing. The bridge was a mecca for the 'spotters' and an excellent viewpoint into the station approaches and north to the lines out of the town. This view is now obscured by the new road development that by-passed the (now closed) level crossing. The footbridge still links Chichester Road to Upper Bognor and London Road but the scene is now more peaceful - and comes with less variety! This is an unknown K, allocated to Three Bridges MPD, and on roster 691, which involved goods trains to Chichester, Barnham and Bognor. The engine would have arrived at lunch-time light engine and after two hours shunting the yard, departed for Three Bridges at 5.0 pm. The fire-man is hard at work adding coal to the firebox and cast-ing a black pall of smoke over the nearby gardens. The Ks were a very attractive L. Bill-ington designed 2-6-0 sadly all were withdrawn in 1962 when the cull of steam elimi-nated whole classes at the stroke of an accountants pen. One was very nearly pre-served by the Bluebell Rail-way but unfortunately funds were not available at the time.*

Terry Cole's Rolling Stock File No. 14

'Emigrant' Push-Pull Trains (1)

In Rolling Stock File No 6 I promised to return to these interesting vehicles and give some more detail. Originally built from 1905 for 'emigrant' traffic the 18 vehicles which remained in 1942 and which had been given new underframes in the 1930s were converted into 9 side corridor push-pull sets. The conversions resulted in 4 different diagrams of Driving Brake 3rds and Trailer Composites as follows:

Original Type	Rebuilt to	New Diagram	Coach Nos.	Sets
5 Thirds	Driving Brake 3rds	101	2641-5	731-5
4 Brake 3rds	Driving Brake 3rds	100	2646-9	736-9
7 Thirds	Trailer Composites	288	4756-62	731-7
2 Composites	Trailer Composites	289	4763-4	738-9

At only 46ft 6in long these were very short vehicles indeed and only seated 14 first and 64 third class passengers. However they proved very useful on quiet branch lines and could be found on all 3 sections of the Southern lasting until around 1960.

Opposite top - Here is Driving Brake 3rd S2646S of set 736 at Tonbridge on 15/8/59. Allocated to the Hawkhurst branch, it was withdrawn in the November of that year. *Photo - David Wigley*

Opposite bottom - The other coach of set 736 was Trailer Composite S4761S seen at the same date and location. This was one of 7 diagram 288 vehicles which started life as full thirds. Converted to Trailer Composites they could be distinguished from diagram 289 in having all compartments of the same width and 4 doors on the corridor side whereas the others had 3. *Photo - David Wigley*

This page - Leaving the bay platform at Midhurst for Petersfield on 27 June 1951 is M7 No. 30049 pushing an 'emigrant' set. The equally spaced doors of the trailer composite indicate this is a diagram 288 ex 3rd. The leading vehicle appears to have two passenger doors on the corridor side which would be diagram 100. If so it is probably set 737 allocated to the branch at that time.

Photo - Terry Cole Collection

EXTRACTS FROM THE SOUTHERN RAILWAY TRAFFIC CONFERENCE MINUTES

Compiled by David Monk-Steel

Whilst it may be simply interesting in itself to provide a few more 'stand-alone' extracts from the minutes, before doing so it would also be appropriate to describe briefly the status, composition and role of the Traffic Officers Conference. The attached sample page from June 1926 gives some idea of those attending together with their respective positions. The running order of the meetings was nearly always set as follows:

Fatal Accidents to Servants of the Company
Train Accidents
Irregularities in Working (mainly Signals Passed at Danger)
Obstructions on the Line (included level-crossing incidents)
Fires on Company Premises
Burglaries on Company Premises
Mishaps to Company Road Vehicles
Compensation Claims (summary)
Demurrage Charges raised against traders on trucks and sheets (summary)
London Goods Cartage (statistics of Depot traffic)
Average loading of wagons and trains (statistics for London Depots only)
London Parcels Cartage (statistics of Depot traffic)
Outstandings (Goods & Parcels) (Summary)
Surplus Cash and Losses in Booking (total)
Fruit Traffic (Seasonal returns of carryings)
Hop Pickers Traffic (Seasonal returns of carryings)
Padstow Fish Traffic (Seasonal returns of carryings)
Cab Privileges (details of changes)
Ledger Accounts (applications for new)
Bad Debts (details)
Engine Failures (Statistics)
Mileage (Statistics of Engines and Trains)
Working of Passenger Trains (Timekeeping statistics)
Continental Traffic (analysis of Passenger and Cargo carried by route)
Isle of Wight Passenger Traffic (Statistics)
Passenger Traffic Between Stations (Statistics Section by Section)
Traffic Receipts (total)
Comparative returns for 'Big Four' (extract from return to BoT)
Special Traffics (e.g. Epsom Races, University Boat Race, Aldershot Military Tattoo etc - passenger returns)
Passenger's Checked Luggage (Summary)
Excess Fares collected (summary)
Salaries & Wages (various tables of amounts paid)
Staff 60 years old or over (list of persons and whether Superannuated or not)
Newspaper Contracts (summary of receipts)
Forged Treasury notes (list of forgeries detected)
Changes to Station Names and Facilities
Post Office Telephone Facilities (detail of new or altered)
Changes to Sidings, and Private Trader agreements (details)

Details of new services to be implemented, and also service withdrawals.
New Works (authorised with cost)
Disposal of Surplus Assets (Authorised with savings / recovery)

The order did flex, and topics were not always discussed at every meeting, particularly if there was nothing to report. There is also a note of separate returns that were submitted but not discussed or not recorded in the minutes, e.g. Staff Punishments

It should also be noted that the Conference was primarily an Operating and Commercial conference, thus generally matters affecting Engineering and Workshops were ignored, unless they impinged upon the Operating Department. During the War the title changed to that of General Manager's Reports and a lot of Workshop matters crept in at the expense of detail in other areas.

Meetings took place ten times a year, every month except May and August, although again this tended to be flexible too, no doubt driven by Officer's holidays!

What is really fascinating is the volume and detail of matters discussed. The Southern Railway consisted of 2,100 route miles, running 6,500 passenger trains daily, and yet seems to have got through this massive agenda every time. I expect they were talking well into the evening (although this isn't recorded of course)!

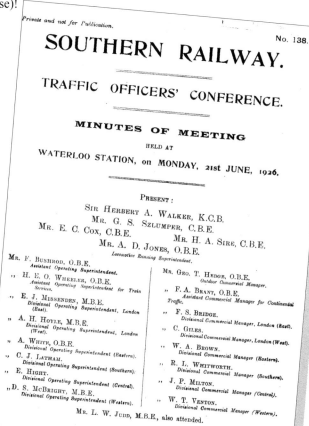

WORKING OF PASSENGER TRAINS APRIL 1935.

a - Statements showing the working of Continental Express trains between London and the Ports Weekdays and Sundays, during the month of April 1935 were submitted.

b - Statements showing the working of Express passenger (weekdays) other than Continental Express trains, between London and important towns during the month of April 1935 were submitted

b - Statements were submitted giving the following results on the working of all steam (except Continental Express trains) and Electric trains on Weekdays and Electric trains on Weekdays and Sundays during the month of April 1935.

STEAM TRAINS - WEEKDAYS

Division		No. of trains run	Trains right time		Trains 1 to 5 minutes late		Trains 6 to 10 minutes late		Trains 11 to 20 minutes late		Trains over 20 minutes late		Average late arrivals during month. Minutes
			Number	% of total	Number	% of total	Number	% of total	Number	% of total	Number	% of total	
London West	1935	12,104	8,556	70.69	2,970	24.54	492	4.06	75	.62	11	.09	1.01
	1934	13,400	9,430	70.38	3,120	23.28	738	5.51	102	.76	10	.07	1.1
Isle of Wight	1935	3,460	2,890	83.55	483	13.96	75	2.17	12	.34	-	-	.55
	1934	3,724	3,063	82.25	574	15.42	79	2.12	8	.21	-	-	.53
London East	1935	15,090	12,294	81.47	2,094	13.88	494	3.27	180	1.19	28	19	.81
	1934	17,497	13,824	79.01	2,823	16.13	647	3.7	175	1	28	.16	.87
London Central	1935	17,310	12,718	73.47	4,038	23.33	468	2.7	76	.44	10	.05	.79
	1934	20,903	16,086	76.95	4,239	20.27	453	2.17	115	.55	10	.05	.69
Southern	1935	7,532	5,091	78.34	1,375	18.26	203	2.7	45	.6	8	.1	.74
	1934	8,452	6,199	73.34	1,859	21.99	287	3.4	92	1.09	15	.18	.99
Western	1935	9,073	8,222	90.62	898	7.69	115	1.27	32	.35	6	.07	.37
	1934	9,852	8,413	85.4	1,129	11.46	219	2.22	77	.78	14	.14	.61
Total for System	1935	64,539	50,581	78.34	11,658	18.05	1,847	2.87	420	.65	63	.09	.75
	1934	73,828	57,015	77.23	13,744	18.62	2,423	3.28	569	.77	77	.1	.82

STEAM TRAINS SUNDAYS

Division		No. of trains run	Number	% of total	Number	% of total	Number	% of total	Number	% of total	Number	% of total	Average
London West	1935	1,228	994	80.95	175	14.25	47	3.83	10	.81	2	.16	.79
	1934	1,278	1,032	80.75	187	14.65	46	3.6	10	.79	3	.23	.82
Isle of Wight	1935	431	349	80.97	60	13.93	17	3.94	5	1.16	-	-	.83
	1934	373	311	83.38	43	11.53	6	2.15	9	2.41	2	.53	.95
London East	1935	1,697	1,434	84.5	186	10.96	52	3.05	21	1.24	4	.24	.79
	1934	1,727	1,382	80.02	253	14.65	51	2.95	39	2.26	2	.12	.89
London Central	1935	1,692	1,203	71.1	364	21.51	86	5.08	35	2.07	4	.24	1.16
	1934	1,975	1,488	75.34	403	20.41	62	3.14	20	1.01	2	.1	.85
Southern	1935	481	353	73.39	86	17.88	19	3.95	17	3.53	6	1.25	1.61
	1934	470	368	78.3	75	15.96	21	4.47	5	1.06	1	.21	.94
Western	1935	270	225	83.34	32	11.85	6	2.22	6	2.22	1	.37	1.02
	1934	305	239	78.36	53	17.38	11	3.6	1	.33	1	.33	.91
Total for System	1935	5,799	4,558	78.6	903	15.57	227	3.92	94	1.62	17	.29	.98
	1934	6,128	4,820	78.53	1,014	16.55	199	3.25	84	1.37	11	.18	.87

ELECTRIC TRAINS - WEEKDAYS

Division		No. of trains run	Number	% of total	Number	% of total	Number	% of total	Number	% of total	Number	% of total	Average
London West	1935	17,134	14,119	82.41	2,822	16.47	181	1.06	11	.06	1	.0	.46
	1934	18,648	15,007	80.48	3,330	17.86	275	1.47	35	.19	1	.0	.53
London East	1935	32,796	26,868	81.92	5,711	17.41	186	.57	28	.09	3	.01	.39
	1934	35,620	28,553	80.16	6,807	19.11	202	.56	38	.11	20	.06	.42
London Central	1935	38,601	30,831	79.87	7,459	19.32	264	.69	42	.11	5	.01	.42
	1934	42,205	33,183	78.62	8,570	20.31	359	.85	79	.19	14	.03	.46
Total for System	1935	88,531	71,818	81.13	15,992	18.06	631	.71	81	.09	9	.01	.41
	1934	96,473	76,743	79.55	18,707	19.39	836	.87	152	.16	35	.03	.46

		ELECTRIC TRAINS - SUNDAYS											
London West	1935	2,705	2,606	93.37	171	6.14	8	.29	-	-	-	-	.15
	1934	2,789	2,492	89.35	262	9.39	25	.9	7	.25	3	.11	.33
London East	1935	5,876	5,210	91.79	443	7.80	19	.33	2	.04	2	.04	.18
	1934	5,677	5,187	91.37	466	8.21	16	.28	8	.14	-	-	.19
London Central	1935	6,348	5,744	90.49	564	8.88	31	.49	9	.14	-	-	.2
	1934	6,349	5,501	86.64	766	12.06	67	1.06	12	.19	3	.05	.35
Total for System	1935	14,809	13,560	91.57	1,178	7.96	58	.39	11	.07	2	.01	.18
	1934	14,815	13,180	88.97	1,494	10.08	108	.73	27	.18	6	.04	.27

DAYS OMITTED

1935 - All Divisions: April 18, 20, 22 and 23 - Easter Period April 19 (Good Friday) treated as additional Sunday.
London Central: April 5, 6, 7 (all steam trains) Southerham Bridge damaged.
1934 - All Divisions: April 2 and 3 - Easter Period.

RYDE PIER HEAD, 6th SEPTEMBER. 1935

At 12.15 a,m. on the 6 September, when Petrol Car No. 2, with Trailer Car No. 4 leading and a luggage trailer being hauled, running empty from Ryde Esplanade, arrived at Ryde Pier Head, the Trailer Car ran through the sand drag at the end of the rails, demolished the stop-blocks and came to rest on the top of the wooden staging which forms the approach to the platform, with its leading end twenty-six feet past the position originally occupied by the stopblocks. The Trailer Car also broke two cast iron pillars supporting the station roof.

No. 4 Trailer Car was damaged beyond repair, whilst the leading end of Petrol Car No. 2 was badly damaged.

A number of passengers were on the platform waiting the arrival of the tram, none of whom was hurt, but two men who were on the steps leading to the platform sustained slight injury.

When a tram is proceeding from the Esplanade to the Pier Head, the driver is sitting with his back towards the direction of travel and there is a post situated between the eastern and western tracks of the tramway about 220 feet from the buffer stops at the Pier Head, which post is provided to enable the Driver to determine his position for the purpose of stopping the car at the platform.

A red lamp is provided, which should be lighted <u>and</u> placed on this post at dusk, but, on the occasion in question, the lamp had not been placed in position consequently Acting Driver Frampton had some difficulty in ascertaining his position. Conductor Attrill, who, according to instructions, should have been at the leading end of the trailer oar No. 4 so as to have been in a position to apply the hand brake when approaching the Pier Head Terminus, was with the Driver and, therefore, not able to give any assistance with regard to stopping the movement.

It was the duty of Acting Driver Frampton to see that the Conductor placed the red lamp in position, and he has been suspended from duty for three days. Conductor Attrill has been cautioned. It transpires that Drivers and Conductors on the Tramway have not been properly supervised by Mr Millichap, the Station Master at Ryde, and suitable notice has been taken of this.

STROOD TUNNEL, BETWEEN HIGHAM AND STROOD, 9 DECEMBER. 1935

On the 9 December, the Length Ganger discovered that a movement of the brickwork had occurred in Strood Tunnel at a point approximately 23 chains from the London end. A speed restriction of 15 miles per hour was at once imposed on Traffic on both lines, and the Engineer was given possession of the lines from 12.45 until 2.45 a.m. on the 10 December to enable an examination to be made, when it was found that a further movement had taken place.

The down and up lines could not be cleared until 5.55 a.m. and 6.40 a.m. respectively, when traffic was resumed subject to a speed restriction of 10 miles per hour.

Whilst the lines were closed a 'bus service was run between Strood and Gravesend Central. Three services were diverted via Swanley, and other trains were terminated at Strood.

The bulge in the brickwork will necessitate the rebuilding of approximately 50 feet of the tunnel wall, and in order to allow of the work being carried out it will be necessary for the roads to be interlaced, and single line working introduced, for which purpose tablet instruments have been installed in Higham and Strood Tunnel Signal Boxes.

It is anticipated that this method of working will probably be necessary for a period of approximately two months, and the train service will be altered as follows:-

1. Electric services will be maintained between Gravesend Central and London.
2. Up steam trains originating at points below Chatham will be retimed earlier in order to effect connections at Gravesend Central.
3. Down steam trains will be maintained as far as possible and suitable arrangements made for ensuring connections at Chatham.

Notes to table on opposite page: EXTENSION OF ELECTRIC SERVICES
1 May 1934 to St Mary Cray.
6 January 1935 to Sevenoaks via Swanley Junction and Orpington.
1934 - Good Friday March 30 - Easter Monday April 2.
1935 - Good Friday April 19.
The trains in the special Bank Holiday working time table have been treated as 'Ordinary', except those booked to run if required, which have been treated as 'Special' if run.

MILES RUN (APRIL 1935) STEAM ENGINE MILES AND HOURS

	MILES		HOURS	
	Current Period	% Increase (+) or Decrease (-)	Current Period	% Increase (+) or Decrease (-)
Coaching (A)				
Train	2,220,406	- 3.11	136,710	- 3.27
Shunting	183,560	- 1.67	36,530	- 1.55
Assisting and Light	118,007	- 16.17	15,737	- 12.55
Total	2,521,973	- 3.71	190,977	- 3.78
Freight				
Train	534,516	+ 3.18	54,232	+ 1.26
Shunting	513,806	+ 1.81	102,474	+ 1.93
Assisting and Light	98.817	+ 1.77	10,179	+ 1.58
Total	1,147,139	+ 2.44	166,905	+ 1.08

(A) Includes Sentinel Car

ELECTRIC CAR MILES (APRIL 1935)

Section of Line	Current Period	(+) Increase (-) Decrease	Aggregate for 16 Weeks	
			Current Period	(+) Increase (-) Decrease
Western (Excluding Waterloo & City)	2,741,190	- 8,587	10,927,776	+ 63,404
Eastern - Central	8,642,591	+ 204,038	34,742,261	+ 1,245,473
Waterloo & City	49,323	+ 4,147	195,667	+ 8.071
Total	11,433,104	+ 199,398	45,865,704	+ 1,316,948

	Current Period	**Corresponding Period Last Year**	**Aggregate for 16 Weeks**		
			Current Period	**Corresponding Period Last Year**	
SENTINEL CAR					
Passenger Loaded	1,282	1,194	8,402	8,318	Note -
Passenger Empty	-	-	2	-	These miles are included on
Departmental	-	207	-	207	the Mileage Summary under
PETROL CARS					the heading 'Steam Locomo-
Passenger Loaded	-	1,100	-	4,660	tive Engines.'
Passenger Empty	-	-	-	-	
Trial Trips	-	-	-	-	
Engineer's Dept.	108	46	304	146	

Miles Run by Southampton Docks Engines

	Current Period	**Corresponding Period Last Year**
Coaching Shunting	2,075	1,930
Freight Shunting	19,555	17,930
Total	21,630	19,860

	Current Period	**Corresponding Period Last Year**
Number of Weekdays	23	22
Number of Sundays *	5	5
Number of Bank Holidays	1	1
Total Number of Days	28	28

*Including Good Friday

SOUTHERN REGION BRITISH RAILWAYS

H. C. LANG Chief Establishment & Staff Officer
G. H. LUCK Asst. Establishment & Staff Officer

Waterloo Station, London, S.E.1
WATerloo 5151 Ext. **2096/2423**
Telegrams: Establishment Waterloo Rail London

11th October, 1963.

S.377/15/82(T)

Dear Mr. Widdowson,

ENQUIRY CLERKS' COURSES

You will have learnt already that you have been selected to attend a 5-day residential Course for Enquiry Clerks at Kingsgate College, Broadstairs, commencing on Monday, 4th November, 1963.

This course is intended to assist you in your duties as an Enquiry Clerk, and will include, among other things, instruction in railway geography, the use of the public and working timetables, service to the travelling public, and methods of dealing with enquiries by telephone and correspondence. Periods will also be devoted to Continental Train and Boat services, reservations, regulations, and Car Ferry Bookings. Enquiry clerks from various parts of the Region and our Continental Offices will attend the course, and you will have the opportunity of discussing with your colleagues, the visiting speakers, and the Course Leader, the various problems arising from your duties.

The Course Leader, Mr. B.W. Murray is a practical railwayman as well as a teacher. He was formerly clerk-in-charge of the Central Telephone Enquiry Bureau at Waterloo Station, and has a useful fund of experience in this field to place at your disposal. I know you will enjoy working with him.

I enclose Joining Instructions and general information about the College; you should receive a pass through normal Departmental channels to cover your journey to Broadstairs and back. I trust that the course should prove instructive and interesting. I trust that the knowledge gained will broaden your outlook and thus help you in tackling your day-to-day duties and problems.

Yours sincerely,

D. WILLEY,
Training & Education Officer

Mr. K. Widdowson,
81 Amchurst Drive,
ST. MARY CRAY,

RESIDENTIAL COURSE FOR ENQUIRY CLERKS
KINGSGATE COLLEGE, BROADSTAIRS

COURSE NO.E.3. WEEK COMMENCING 4TH NOVEMBER, 1963

LIST OF STUDENTS

1. ABURROW, M. — Bognor Regis.
2. COLDWELL, E. — Eastbourne
3. MORGAN, T.A. — Brighton
4. CAMPBELL-MARSHALL, P.C. — B.R. Office, Paris.
5. SPARROW, Mrs. A. — Salisbury
6. HANCOX, B. — Southampton Central
7. HANNING, J.F. — Southampton Central
8. WIDDOWSON, K. — Travel Facilities L.M.O. (S.W.) Waterloo.
9. LIPS, Miss M. — B.R. Office, Bale.
10. ILLUKIEWITZ, Miss K. — Continental Enquiry Office, Victoria.
11. FOSTER, J.R. — Continental Enquiry Office, Victoria.
12. SQUIRES, I.W. — Dumpton Park
13. LESSITER, Mrs. M. — Sevenoaks
14. HARRIS, Miss G.M. — L.M.O. (.S.W.) Wimbledon.
15. WELSTEAD, Miss L.M. — L.M.O. (S.W.) Wimbledon.
16. CHARMAN, R.J.K. — Bournemouth West.

GRATUITOUS

Passenger Services Timetable

MAIN LINE AND SUBURBAN

LONDON
Victoria
Waterloo
Charing Cross
London Bridge
Cannon Street
Holborn Viaduct
and the
SOUTH-EAST
SOUTH & WEST
OF ENGLAND

9th SEPTEMBER 1963 to 14th JUNE 1964 (or until further notice)

Supplements, giving details of alterations to this timetable, are issued free of charge see page 2.

British Railways
SOUTHERN REGION

"HELLO, TRAIN ENQUIRIES - HOW CAN I HELP YOU?"

Keith Widdowson

The editor's appeal for stories about railway office life (Issue 11) triggered memories of my time in the CTEB (Central Telephone Enquiry Bureau) at Waterloo. Located 'in the gods' on the 4th floor of the General Manager's Offices, a panoramic view of London was available to the north whilst the south alignment, courtesy of the station's 21 platform glass roof, kindly (not!) ensured that during the summer the office became akin to an unbearable sweat box. Although administratively allied to the South Western Division, we at Waterloo were *THE* Southern Region enquiry office, the telephone number of which, if my memory serves me correctly, was Waterloo (later 01 928) 5100. The only access to the forth floor was from the centrally positioned lift, the entrance to which was adjacent to the carriageway arch opposite Waterloo Eastern. This, however, was locked after normal office hours, resulting in a long trek through darkened and quiet corridors - buzzing with 'suits and secretaries' during the day - to the manned entrance opposite Platform 2 and was necessary when either taking a break or after completion of duties in the evenings / weekends. No door-entry system or ID card authorisation was insisted upon in those days.

Aged just 15 in 1962, and a newcomer to the world of work, the benefits of conversing with intending passengers with their differing dialects and varying aspects of politeness (or not). I believe my time in the CTEB helped me to become increasingly confident in dealing with 'strangers': in this case members of the public by phone. My designated position was actually in the adjacent Travel Facilities section, which dealt with the correspondence side of customer's travel enquires. I was, therefore, effectively a relief clerk within the bureau and only utilized during 'emergency' times i.e. staff shortages, service disruptions (weather / derailments / strikes etc) and as such was, on such occasions, effectively always thrown in at the deep end.

The opportunity for overtime was often offered and eagerly taken up – my normal take home wage being £2 12s 6d. Taking into consideration the shift patterns, I must admit I was grateful not to be a permanent member of the section - it being manned 24/7 all year, with in those days BR operating services on Christmas Day.

The following year, 1963, the chance came to attend a week-long residential course at Broadstairs, specifically aimed at new clerks on BR who regularly dealt with the public. The excitement of living away from home for the first time was tempered by the promised lengthy work sessions (see timetable) filling both each day and my head with all the different aspects the public might require. Spoof customers (in reality volunteer BR managers) were set up to ask, nay - demand, a range of transport related enquiries. We were taught never to lose our tempers no matter how baited we were and to placate even the most complaining passenger. It was said that with all necessary publications i.e. fares books / timetables / maps to hand, there should not have been any unanswerable questions being asked – some hope! The evenings were spent learning the craft of dart throwing in a nearby pub…also having to cope with a new fangled-scoring machine!

In February 1966 and with by then an increasing realisation that the operating rather than commercial aspects of BR were of more interest, I obtained promotion to the South Eastern Division, then located at Queen Street in the City, as a journal marker. Further moves to the DMO at Wimbledon occurred before returning to Waterloo for a position within the Central Crew Diagrams office, again located on the 4th floor and, would you believe it, slap bang next to the CTEB.

By this time and having exhausted the British steam scene, travels further afield to Europe were costing a considerable amount of money, thus the welcome chance to work overtime within the CTEB, when offered, was once more eagerly accepted. (My first book *The Great Iron Horse Chase: Europe* depicts those travels through Europe during 1968/9). A normal Sunday for me was either a day shift on my regular job within train planning, or the lunchtime session as a barman at my local pub, before working a 15 30 to 23 30 shift on the phones. My 'Sunday roast' was enjoyed at a nearby café at the Bullring at approximately 19 00 hours – the site now a bus station and a multiplex cinema. Regular members of the CTEB used to swap with me when allocated this particular shift, because of their inability to get home – I had a 23 36 Waterloo (Eastern) to Petts Wood and a two mile walk. This arrangement continued into the early 1970s because, whilst I no longer followed steam the costs associated with car ownership and courting were just, if not greater, than before.

Anyway I digress, so back to the CTEB. As a hormonal teenager, if given the opportunity, I usually chose to sit next to one of the few young girls (there being an otherwise high average age amongst the workforce), some of whom, when perched on their swivel seats and with mini skirts in fashion, showed some glorious expanses of leg, sufficient to distract me enough to ask the caller to repeat their request. In times of service disruption caused by fog, snow, derailments or strikes, as many as 60 calls per hour were being answered by each of us. Most a simple enquiry with the caller asking the time of the next train. But with sometimes sparse information filtering through from the three control offices - their priority being to get the trains running rather than disseminating the results - we just didn't know, so we advised passengers to turn up and wait – having checked that at least a skeleton service WAS running on the line in question. The numbers of calls waiting were monitored by a machine, equipped with a cylindrical drum and an arrow, located above the supervi-

Opposite far left, top and bottom - *A promise of excitement, or so I thought, away from home.*
Opposite near left, top - *Top right - 4th floor corridor at Waterloo, Full of 'Suits and secretaries' during the daytime.*
Opposite near left , bottom - *Our bible, notice the 'Gratuitous' heading.*

ENQUIRY CLERKS' COURSE - KINGSGATE COLLEGE, BROADSTAIRS

	MONDAY	TUESDAY	WEDNESDAY	THURSDAY	FRIDAY
9.15 a.m.		HOW TO GET THE BEST OUT OF PEOPLE - Group discussion on mass public behaviour BWM	YOUR CUSTOMER AND YOU - The importance of speech, personality and dress - Tape recording session. BWM	CONTINENTAL ENQUIRIES - Routes, Timetables, Fares, Bookings, Reservations, and Currency Regulations. Visiting Speaker HAF	COMMUNICATIONS - Letter writing, the of the telephone, th importance of good relationships B
	10.45a.m. - 11.15a.m. Morning Coffee (11.00a.m.)				
1.15a.m.	COURSE ASSEMBLES On arrival course members are asked to complete a questionnaire, and after an interview with the Course Leader will be allocated to either 'A' or 'B' class	(A) SPECIAL NOTICES Fog, Ice, and Snow GSU (B) PUBLIC TIMETABLES (Contd.) L.T.E. London Conntns. BWM	PUBLIC ENQUIRIES - By telephone and correspondence - Visiting Speaker JBE	GENERAL FACILITIES Fares, Excursions, Road/Rail/Air Facilities, Seat and Sleeper bookings Visiting Speaker WC/DV	REQUEST AND REVISION PERIOD / OPEN FORUM
	12.45p.m. - 2.15p.m. Lunch (1.00p.m.)				
2.15p.m.	INTRODUCTION TO COURSE / SERVICE TO THE PUBLIC Discussion and film-strip BWM	(A) CROSS COUNTRY & AWKWARD TABLES BWM (B) THE S.R. SUBURBAN TIMETABLE GSU	(A) GUIDED TIMETABLE EXERCISES BWM (B) GUIDED TIMETABLE EXERCISES GSU	TRAVEL AGENTS - How they serve the public and the railways Visiting Speaker SDH	KEY — BWM B.W. Murray (Course Leader); GSU G.S. Uzzell (Instructor)
	3.45p.m. - 4.15p.m. - Afternoon Tea (4.00p.m.)				
4.15p.m.	GEOGRAPHY - The S.R. Network GSU	MOCK ENQUIRY OFFICE Counter exercises (Southampton Ctl.)	MOCK ENQUIRY OFFICE Counter exercises (East Croydon)	MOCK ENQUIRY OFFICE - Counter exercises (Ashford, Kent)	JBE J.B. Ede (Clerk in Charge C.T.B. Waterloo); A.T. A. Thomas (Car Ferry Cent); H.A.F H.A. Flood (Ship.& Contl.D)
	5.45p.m. - 7.00p.m. - Dinner (6.00p.m.)				
7.00p.m.	(A) WORKING TIMETABLES GSU (B) PUBLIC TIMETABLES Their structure and use BWM	FILM SHOW (optional)	CAR FERRY TRAFFIC - Bookings, Regulations, and General Facilities Visiting Speaker AT	MOCK ENQUIRY OFFICE - Team Competition. (LONDON)	W.C. W. Crump L.M.O. Ctl.; D.V. D. Vine L.M.O. Ctl.; SDH S. DeHaan (Travel Agent)

sors desk who, having noted any clerk 'wasting time' (chatting or drinking tea), would shout up the office – "get answering …".

Boat trains from Southampton were highlighted on a chalked board (as indeed were any disruptions to traffic) at one end of the office, their arrival times being updated, as facts became known. With most voyages originating from across the Atlantic, sea conditions could play havoc with the scheduled arrival time, sometimes by as much as several days. Distraught relations of the wave of West Indians, lured here with promised employment, often slept on the Waterloo concourse whilst awaiting their loved ones.

Train service alterations, such as engineering works or race days at Ascot, Sandown, and Goodwood etc, were always shown within publications called Special Traffic Notices. That was fine if each of the three divisions worked to a standard format – but no. Perhaps attempting to retain some individuality left over from pre-grouping days, each one was differently laid out, a nightmare to unravel when callers were impatiently 'put on hold'. Regular off-peak services did not need reference to the well thumbed timetable, ie every hour on the hour from Charing Cross to the Kent Coast and Victoria to Brighton, with the added warning not to travel on certain departures to the latter, unless you are prepared to pay the supplement for the 'Brighton Belle'. The irregular Bournemouth and West of England departures did, however, need more attention, particularly if they were travelling onto the sparsely served 'Withered Arm'.

Suburban travellers were dealt with easily on off peak enquiries, but the immensely complex rush hour workings had to be minutely examined before dissemination. When asked about other regions' train services, we were told to refer the caller to the appropriate regional bureau, although taking into consideration my burgeoning nationwide knowledge, I could often unofficially help, but at the same time asking the caller to double check in case of, unbeknown to us, engineering works affected their journey.

The regular clerks had their own desks (40 plus seats) and, subject to their shifts, when I worked overtime I sat in the vacant chair. Woe betide leaving it untidy for their following duty. A eclectic mix of personages were employed, from those who had been in the bureau all their working life, to retired managers unable to exist without something to do. We also had employees taken off the track with medical problems or perhaps because of domestic issues, unable to work night shifts. Most of the bus timetables for the south of England were similarly held in the office, East Kent, Southdown, Western National amongst them. All were necessary, as to get the caller to their final destination with Dr Beeching continually trimming the network was sometimes quite tricky. Tea was provided every hour on the hour – the clerk designated grateful for the time away from, in busy times, a continuous demand for information. The mess room was just across the corridor and 2 x 15 minute breaks, in addition to a 1-hour meal break, were awarded to each 8-hour shift. Needless to say there were no smoking restrictions anywhere, either at your work desk or in the mess room.

So that perhaps sums up the working ethic of the bureau. When times were a little less stressed and taking into account the nature of the caller (after experience you can always tell within a few words how a caller might react to a little jesting), a little fun could be had. Often leaving our answers open to deliberate misinterpretation. Questions then, such as the following, were often replied to:

Q - "*How long is the next train to Portsmouth?*" A - "They are all 12 coaches madam!"

Q - "*When is the first train to Bournemouth tomorrow (perhaps expecting a breakfast time departure)?*" A - "02 45 sir!"

Q - "*Can I get to the south coast WITHOUT going through a tunnel because I am claustrophobic?*" A - The answer was surprisingly "'No".

Q - "*I don't know Waterloo station very well, how will I find the taxis / tube?*" A - "I could meet you under the big clock and show you around." (Only applicable to young sounding females!)

The chief clerk, aware of my steam interest, often highlighted unusual workings involving steam for me on the stencil issued special traffic notices. These notices were full of train alterations that had missed the printed weekly issues. On such working was the 17 20 London Bridge to Brighton (via Oxted) which reverted to steam haulage for a short period of time - I think November 1963. Although I went and watched it depart, I stupidly never travelled on it (I believe it was an Unmodified Pacific), instead dutifully going home just a few minutes late for my evening meal so as not to worry my parents unnecessarily. How times change, within a year I was hardly ever at home during daylight hours for months on end, let alone the hundreds of nights spent chasing steam workings during the last few years of their existence.

Later on in the early 1980s, the bureau was relocated down in the depths of Waterloo station, the reason being that the Train Planning Office I worked in was expanded to take in staff from the three divisions, aka Network South East.

BRITISH RAILWAYS : SOUTHERN REGION

INQUIRY CLERKS' COURSES
KINGSGATE COLLEGE, BROADSTAIRS

ARRIVAL: Kingsgate College is about two miles from Broadstairs and students should travel to Broadstairs Station. The No. 49 bus leaves a stop near the Post Office opposite the approach road to the up side of the station. Travel in the direction of Margate and ask for Kingsgate College, the first request stop past Reading Street. Taxis are available at the station.

Students should try to arrive at the college by 12.0 noon on the first day of the course in order to settle in and be ready for lunch at 1.0 p.m.

ACCOMMODATION: is mainly in single rooms, students should bring their own soap, towels are provided. It would be appreciated if students would kindly make their own beds. Shoe cleaning materials, irons and ironing boards are provided in the Cloakroom.

MEAL TIMES: Breakfast   8.30 a.m.
               Lunch   1.0 p.m.
               Tea   4.0 p.m.
               Dinner   6.0 p.m.

Refreshments (Tea and biscuits) are available at 11.0 a.m. and 9.30 p.m.

ELECTRIC RAZORS: The voltage at the College is 230 A.C., plugs for razors are not fitted, but an adaptor can be borrowed on application to the office, deposit 2/0d.

DRESS: Gentlemen should wear a lounge suit for dinner in the evening. Sports clothes may be worn, if desired, at other times.

NEWSPAPERS: A copy of each of the main national daily papers will be found in the Reading Room.

Extra papers may be ordered by signing the lists on the Notice Board in the Hall.

SHOP: The shop, at which stationery, stamps, cigarettes and chocolate etc. may be purchased, is in the office and is open from 9.0 a.m. - 1.0 p.m. and 1.45 p.m. - 2.0 p.m. on weekdays.

TELEPHONE: There is a call box for the use of students under the stairs in the hall. The number is -

THANET 62303

The office number is THANET 61903.

TAXIS: Taxis may be ordered by telephoning THANET 61466, or 61154. When ordering, please give your name in order to avoid confusion between several bookings from the college.

POSTAL INFORMATION:

The correct address is -

Kingsgate College,
Convent Road,
Broadstairs,
Kent.

Happy days indeed and at the get-together at the BRSA Club at Vauxhall in 1997 to mark the offices cessation, privatisation meant the bureau (or call centre as it became known) was outsourced to a company at Cardiff, subsequently India,. It brought home to the attendees how times had changed, not necessarily better, for either staff or passengers 'customers' in today's scenario. I'm just glad I was part of a unified nationalised system to which many thousands of railwaymen did their very best to ensure the travelling public got to where they wanted to go.

Above - *Course attendees at Broadstairs. Apart from myself, back row fourth from right, G Uzzell is front row fourth from left and B Murray on his right.*

Left - *A Brownie 127 shot on 8 December 1963 taken at Hastings and showing No. DS237 'Maunsell' en route from Eastleigh to Ashford. This was only known about resulting from the CETB Supervisor, Wally Hieron, knowing of my interest in steam and highlighting the move on the short notice stencil sheets.*

- and speaking of Waterloo, another Henry Meyer's wonderful images sometime between February and 1 March 1951. (The dates being those when the engine entered traffic and was subsequently named.)

'REBUILT'-THE LETTERS AND COMMENTS PAGE(S)

The subject of wheel-tapping on the Southern region certainly appears to have tapped a few memories (ooh-sorry about that). In all seriousness, we are delighted to continue the theme with this from Mark Brinton, "In Southern Way 11 you request information on Wheel Tappers. I worked for the Southern Region's CM&EE Department at Salisbury from 1978 to 1982 and had colleagues who undertook 'wheel tapping' on rolling stock. The wheel tapping was part of an in service examination of vehicles passing between the Southern and Western regions and was done on most Waterloo to Exeter and Portsmouth to Bristol trains. At the time, these services were mostly formed of vacuum braked Mark 1 stock and therefore not necessarily as well-maintained as more modern vehicles. The purpose of 'wheel tapping' is to detect loose tyres. To achieve a valid response from the wheels the train brakes must be released. Therefore this should only be done where the track is level (although the loco was not subject to wheel tapping and therefore could have its brakes on). Also the train had to be stationary long enough for all the vehicles to be done (usually only on one side). The important parts of the 'in service' examination was to detect anything loose, broken or hanging down, overheating axleboxes etc. wheel tapping was done as an extra check by this time.

"The proper name for 'wheel tappers' was Carriage and Wagon Examiners or later Rolling Stock Technicians. Generally, the routine tapping of wheels in service was slowly phased out with the introduction of scheduled maintenance of rolling stock in the early 1970s. This replaced a previous system of adhoc examination and repairs and led to a significant improvement in stock reliability and reduction in the number of loose tyres and dragging brakes (the cause of most loose tyres). A system of painting markings on wheels was also introduced which allowed shifted tyres to be detected visually, even if they were not loose at the time of inspection. At Salisbury, the tapping of wheel generally ceased with the take-over of the West of England sets by Mark 2 air-braked stock which was considered generally to be in better condition than the older Mark 1 vehicles.

"With regard to 'wheel tapping' in Third-Rail areas, Waterloo had C&W Examiners that also looked at the Waterloo-Exeter stock and often carried a 'tapping' hammer which was useful for other things; however they did not routinely tap wheels as part of their examination of the vehicles, when I knew them.

"In-service inspections were normally undertaken from the 'ground' (non-platform) side so staff would not normally be very visible. If time allowed and having done the 'ground' side, the platform side would be done to check for broken springs etc. Normally at Salisbury the platform side would be checked by standing at the end of the platform as the train ran in. The Examiner would then walk forward along the 'ground' side to the front of the train checking the underside in more detail (and tapping the wheels) as they went.

"The mid-journey in-service inspections at Salisbury were for two main reasons. The first being concern over excessive delays a vehicle defect could cause on the single line to Exeter. The other was the number of vehicles received from the WR which had bits hanging down that caused tripping of the conductor rail supply and resulting damage and delay. Having provided staff (which also included loco fitters) for these reasons, it made

sense to utilise them fully in inspecting other services when not otherwise occupied.

"On another subject, in Martin Breakespear's article on the Southern Pneumatic Pull-Push System there is also a Dennis Callender photo which shows the inside of the driving compartment of Set 503 (4167). This was the IOW PP set which had one on the driving windows blanked off, an exterior view of which featured on the front cover of SW10. With regard to Gerry Bixley's comment in SW11, it can be seen from the Dennis Callender view that the glazing was not just painted over, but the window hole was actually boarded up and presumably the outer metal skin applied to maintain the weather seal. Unfortunately the photo only shown a portion of the 'boarded up' window, but there is visible over the guard's shoulder what appears to be a brake gauge and also a stencilled 'Test the Brake' notice which would suggest the adjacent location of the Guard's brake test cock. Unlike other similar vehicles on the mainland, this one had Westinghouse air brakes rather than the Vacuum system. This would have required a different driver's brake valve and gauges. The boarding-up could be related to the provision of this different

The Dennis Callender view referred to in the text by Mark Brinton. Dennis's records refer to the location as being one of several taken on the Ventnor West line, but without date or exact location.

equipment, however why the PP Brake Composite (6987) and Set 504's BT (4169) did not require it, despite presumably having the same gear, is open to debate.

"I would suspect that Viv's comment regarding the lamp brackets is correct as despite the vehicle being fitted with electric head lights (presumably powered by the coach lighting system), an oil tail light (as in SW10 Cover photo) was used as these were more reliable.

"I would take issue with Martin's statement that the SR did not allow PP vehicles to be coupled either side of the loco and that the Control Cock was fitted to prevent this. It is obvious from the number of photos in existence that the SR did not prohibit this practice and certainly on the IOW the Ventnor West branch regularly operated with PP vehicles on both sides of the loco. The vehicle to the rear of the loco (in direction of travel) did not need to use the PP equipment until the train reversed. I would suggest that normal operation under these circumstances would be to have both sets fully coupled to the loco. The Control Cock being used to select which end would be supplying the Regulator Control Air. Any system leakage, leak-by or unauthorised operation of the trailing end equipment would not then affect the regulator cylinder operation.

"I would also challenge Martin's description of the function of the Release Valve. It is unlikely that any water would have propagated through the system this far and if it did it would collect in the cylinder as this was mounted lower than the Release Valve (according to the drawing mentioned below). I would suspect that its true function was to ensure a rapid exhausting of the regulator cylinder to ensure that the loco regulator closed effectively.

"With regard to the operating pressures, I would suggest that as the system came from the Central Section, where it was originally used with air-braked Brighton locos, the Main Reservoir Pressure would have been the same as used for the brake system, which would have been 70 or 90 psi depending on the type of driver's brake valve fitted. I have checked Eastleigh drawing E-13677 which was prepared for fitting air operated Push & Pull Gear to O2 locos Nos. 188 & 209 for the IOW. This confirms that for air braked locos, the main reservoir was the same as used for the brake system (90psi as brake feed valves were fitted). Unfortunately it does not specify settings for the Reducing Valve or the Release Valve. I hope that you find some of the above useful."

From Alastair Wilson, a very prompt response to the illustration of the 'Lord Nelson' on the Royal working: page 51 of Issue no. 13. "I believe I can make a fair guess at the date and approximate time of the photograph. The clues are as follows:

1. The photograph itself: the head board has the national flags of Canada and the USA, as well as the Union flag. This indicates quite definitely that this was a working associated with the visit of their Majesties King George VI and Queen Elizabeth in the summer of 1939. They left London on Saturday 6th May and returned on Thursday 22nd June.

2. They sailed for Canada from Portsmouth on 6th May, but returned to Southampton on 22nd June. (The dates are confirmed by the Court Circular in 'The Times' for the 8th May and 23rd June.)

3. If the location is at Fleet (and it certainly isn't east of Woking – no conductor rails, and the signal gantry in the background says Basingstoke-Woking), then one might say that the occasion is more likely to have been on the return journey. However, it is possible that they made the outward journey via Basingstoke, Eastleigh and Fareham to Portsmouth, to avoid interfering too much with the regular interval services on the Portsmouth line.

4. The Court Circular gives no indication of the timing of the outward journey, but it was a formal occasion, their Majesties driving in semi-state landaus from Buckingham Palace to Waterloo, where they were seen off by the Prime Minister, several cabinet ministers, the Chairman of the London County Council and the Mayor of Lambeth, a couple of Ambassadors or High Commissioners and members of the Royal family. The Court Circular lists nine other members of the Royal family on the train, as well as Their Majesties, which matches the caption's notation of eleven members on board. They all left the train at Portsmouth and Southsea, where Their Majesties were met by the Lord Lieutenant of Hampshire and the Lord Mayor of Portsmouth. They walked to the Guildhall, inspected a guard of honour, had the keys of the Fortress of Portsmouth presented (and returned) then drove to the Dockyard, where they were greeted by the Commander-in-Chief (and old Uncle Tom Cobley and all), before going on board the Canadian Pacific liner *Empress of Australia*. The Royal Yacht, then the old *Victoria and Albert*, was only fit for short sea passages, not a North Atlantic crossing. On other such occasions, it was usual for them to travel in a Royal Navy warship, but the visit was being made in their capacity as King and Queen of Canada, not as King-Emperor of the British Empire, and so it was thought appropriate that they should travel in a Canadian ship.

All this suggests that the departure from London was not earlier than about 11.00, so if the train travelled via Basingstoke, it would have been passing Fleet at about 11.45. It may be suggested that the light on the train is suitable for a westward-going train, any time after about mid-day.

5. The return on 22nd June took place at some time in the afternoon. The Court Circular records that the *Empress of Britain* (they came back in another Canadian Pacific liner) "arrived at Southampton this afternoon". (The Royal party would have had lunch on board, which suggests it would have been about 14.00 when she berthed.) There was the same formal welcome – much the same players as before, except that the Mayor of Southampton replaced the Lord Mayor of Portsmouth, and they drove to the Civic Centre for presentations, then down to "the Central Railway Station" after inspecting another guard of honour. So it may be suggested that their train didn't leave much before 16.00, and would have been at Fleet at about 16.45. If that were the case, then the photograph, taken from the north side of the line, would have been taken into the sun, which would have been behind the train, and the headboard would have been in shadow, as would the whole of the photographer's side of the train.

So, 6th May, on the outward journey, but going "the wrong way", or homeward bound, on the 22nd June, on the recognised route? Does anyone have the Special Notices for these workings? Because of the light, I favour the outward journey, but, would a 'Nelson' have managed 85 mph on the rising grades to Basingstoke? Not too much problem on the inward run – the load would have been around 200 tons.

A three-pipe problem, my dear Watson!"

From Fred Emery, reference the view of the early LSWR vehicles as appeared at the top of page 4, Issue 10. "The view I think is an early Leyland and an early example of a swap-body. That to the right a stillage to carry the load in the yard and also used for actual loading. I would imagine this to be a publicity photograph as I would think the laden body would require more than two men to roll it forward from the stillage. The chains hanging down are probably the security devices for the load and body. Credence to the publicity theory also comes from the LSWR lettering on the load sheet - rather neat and perhaps deliberately arranged for the photographer.

"In the background, twixt the building and the sheeted load, are some horse-drawn carts, similar to those on pages 48-49 (issue 10) which incidentally have the inscription of 'South Western Railway' when normally 'L.S.W.R' or 'L. &. S.W.R.' was used. Dugald Drummond tried at one time to refer to the company as the 'SWR', in fact a few of his locomotives were turned out lettered that way, but this was frowned on by the directors and he was requested (ordered?) to letter them all with the full initials. Was this even a legal requirement?

"Returning to road vehicles again, the lower image on page 4 (issue 10) would appear to be of new construction despite its solid tyre appearance. Note the 'newness' of the exhaust system. It would appear to be a red chassis and wheels together with a very ornate lining out of the body and cab - even the louvres on the bonnet appear to have white edges, or is this a trick of the sunlight? The lettering is also shaded on the body and cab sides. The canvas screen for use in cold weather is noteworthy as are the solid wheels / tyres which would have given the vehicle a reduced speed as distinct from pneumatically fitted types.

"Two types of lighting are fitted. Oil lamps as side lights and electric headlights, the combination not uncommon in those days of inefficient batteries and dynamos, coupled with the legal requirement for lighting during the hours of darkness.

"Now a comment on Terry Cole's *Rolling-Stock Files* from the same issue. The lower view on page 50 is of a mail van at Wimbledon. The comment is made of the 'Emergency Control Train', at the time of the illustrations there were several time-expired or elderly vehicles at Wimbledon as temporary office accommodation and storage due to bombing in WW2 having caused much damage to the infrastructure, I would suggest this is probably being used as such rather than as part of an emergency rake. "

Gerry Bixley continues on the theme of what he refers to as 'Runways and Demountable Flats', "Just as the Southern Railway produced diagrams for their locos, carriages and wagons, so they produced diagrams for their road vehicle fleets. These brief notes come courtesy of the late Ray Chorley and also Alan Blackburn.

"The LSWR instituted a scheme for the movement of goods around Nine Elms goods depot using old horse-drawn carts adapted with runways on the platform which could carry wheeled demountable flat bodies. These could be loaded directly from rail wagons, then drawn by horse to a free area to await the next available motor lorry. The lorries were also mounted with runways and could be coupled to the carts to the allow the demountable to be transferred to them. The motor lorry could make its delivery and the empty cart re-loaded with an empty (or loaded presumably) demountable. De-mountable lorry bodies are still in use today so the idea may well be nearly 100 years old.

"We know of two types of demountable, Diagram RV41: a 2-ton 6-wheel version, and Diagram RV42: a 4½ ton 8-wheel. Both ran on a track of 3 x 2½" and there were two different sizes of lorry used for their conveyance. By 1934 there were 48 of type RV41 (Nos 1601-48M) and 95 of type RV42 (Nos. 1901-69 / 71-2 / 2034-40 / (210?)1-15 / 7/ 8 M.

"The motor lorries were of Karrier CY or Thorneycroft BT or A2 type for the 2-ton transportables, and AEC, Thorneycroft J, or Karrier make for the 4 / 4½ ton type. Some sample diagrams are reproduced below and opposite:"

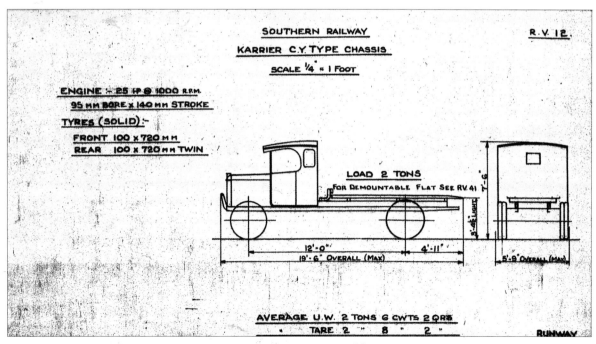

SOUTHERN RAILWAY

KARRIER C.Y. TYPE CHASSIS

SCALE ¼ = 1 FOOT

R.V.12.

ENGINE :- 25 HP @ 1000 R.P.M.

95 MM BORE x 140 MM STROKE

TYRES (SOLID) :-

FRONT 100 x 720 MM

REAR 100 x 720 MM TWIN

LOAD 2 TONS

FOR DEMOUNTABLE FLAT SEE RV.41

12'-0"   4'-11"

19'-6" OVERALL (MAX)   5'-9" OVERALL (MAX)

AVERAGE U.W. 2 TONS 6 CWTS 2 QRS

TARE 2 " 8 " 2 "

RUNWAY

More on the topic of road vehicles, plus further diagrams will appear in SW15.

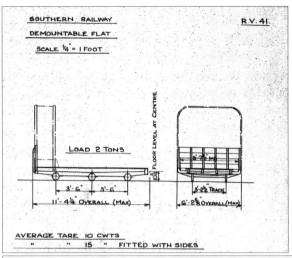

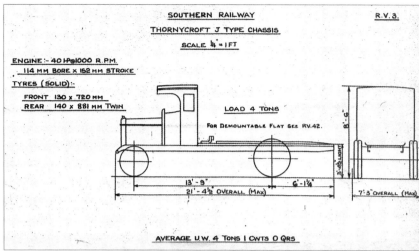

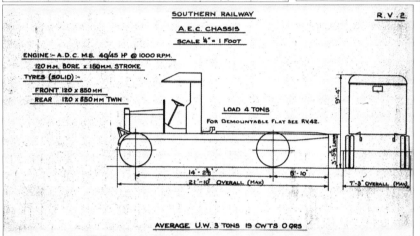

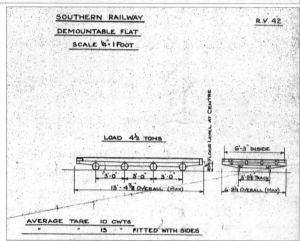

Now to return to the topic of 'Woking Homes', another subject which has contributed much to the postbag of late. Mr Tom Henningsen - whose own memories of East Grinstead Ticket Office appeared in Issue 13, was involved with fundraising for Woking from 1952, and may be best described in his own words. "My association with the Woking homes dates back to 1952 when I joined the Railway service. I started at Clapham Junction, then the clerical training centre, and upon completion of the course was posted to East Grinstead ticket office. The stationmaster very quickly introduced me to the 1d paybill deduction, I was unaware there were any 2d or 3d deductions.

"In 1953 I was asked by a passenger if I could track down a raincoat he had left on a main line Brighton train. I located it at Preston Park and had it returned to me. I was to learn there was a valuable piece of dental equipment in the pocket. The passenger was so grateful that he left me with a large donation for a railway charity. I sent this to Woking Homes and duly received a receipt from Mr Evershed together with a packet of 'Bic' pens for sale on his behalf! He never missed a trick and in consequence so started my support for the Homes, which still continues to this day. (Tom continues with details of his involvement at the Home, first as a part time financial advisor and later as a fund raiser, both locally and then from his home in Cornwall.)

This page - three items recently received. Top is Michael Harvey at Three Bridges panel (see SW No. 12). Michael comments, *"These were part of a series taken by the railway in connection with a series of safety posters being produced. The images of me were not used although those of one of my colleagues were."*

Above - From Bill Jackson. *"The Riverside Meadows in Guildford run alongside the River Wey. Under the viaduct (known locally as The Seven Arches) which carries the Guildford New-Line over the river is a council run car-park. These photos show a train on top of the height barrier to the car-park, the arches mirroring those of the adjacent viaduct. The wagon loads represent creatures etc displayed alongside the riverside walk. The work is by Richard Farrington and supported Rushmon Homes. Photos by Footloose Wines.."*

Opposite page - Recently received from Roger Jones of Newbury are the two views opposite. They form part of a collection of what are believed to be mainly Kent village and country scenes, the majority in print form, but with a few, like that at the bottom, as a glass negative. None have any annotation, hence the question does anyone have any ideas where?

Top - Hayling Island *trains ran through an open landscape of meadows and arable land interspersed with gorse, hawthorn and scrub oak. 'Terrier' tank No. 32650 heads a Bank Holiday service with a BR suburban coach and two Maunsells.*

Bottom - Havant *was the junction station for Hayling Island services with the LB&SCR and L&SWR. Passengers are already boarding this train as No. 32677 is uncoupled prior to running round. The three 'Terriers' in this tribute are:*

BR	LB&SCR	Built	Photographed	Withdrawn	Fate
32650	50 Whitechapel	1876	1961	1964	*Preserved on the K&ESR*
32661	61 Sutton	1875	1961	1963	*Scrapped*
32677	77 Wonersh	1880	1958	1959	*Scrapped*

During the 1930s / 40s, Whitechapel and Wonersh served on the Isle of Wight with different numbers and names.

ON BRIGHTON LINES:
THE FINAL WISPS OF STEAM

Alan Postlethwaite

Introduction: Some four decades after the Grouping, whole trains of the London, Brighton & South Coast Railway were still in regular service. Between 1958 and 1963, the author was fortunate to have the opportunity to photograph some of them before they became extinct. There were also hybrid trains with locomotives or rolling stock from the Southern and BR eras as well as foreigners who had wandered in from the SE&CR, L&SWR and LMS. This article is a celebration of those historic final few years of steam on the Brighton system.

Hayling Island was the last preserve of class A1X 'Terrier' tanks in BR passenger service. Of the fifty introduced in 1872 by Stroudley, twenty-two were reboilered from 1911 by Marsh. At the Hayling terminus, loco coal is being stacked on the wooden staithe while a young couple inspect the diminutive No. 32661. It was a magical place.

Right - The line from *Ryde St Johns Road* to *Ryde Pierhead* was jointly owned by the LB&SCR and L&SWR. In 1958, St Johns was home to one of the last survivors of Brighton class E1 tank - once used for heavy freight and for 'Tourist Specials' to Ventnor, Newport and Freshwater. Introduced in 1874 by Stroudley, 72 were built until 1883. No. 3 Ryde was formerly No. 154 Madrid. It was refitted with a Marsh boiler and transferred to the Isle of Wight in 1932.

Top - The LB&SCR had a multitude of secondary routes between London and Brighton. The westernmost ran via Horsham and Shoreham. Departing **Partridge Green**, L&SWR class M7 tank No. 30049 propels a push-pull train southwards.

Bottom - Another interloper, this time SE&CR class H tank No. 31543 at **Cranleigh** on the Horsham to Guildford line. Note the neatly-clipped hedge and the LB&SCR wooden signal post with SR arms. The leading coach is an SE&CR ten-compartment third, here augmenting a Maunsell push-pull set but originally used for sardine commuting to London.

*Maunsell engines from the inter-war years (both 0-6-0 and 2-6-0) handled much of the heavy freight latterly along the South Coast. At **Lewes**, class Q No. 30533 hauls a fitted freight onto the Haywards Heath line, bound for Bricklayers Arms. Lewes always had spectacular signalry. In this composition, we find 8 starting signals and 4 shunting signals from the Southern era as well as a water crane, a flower tub, a signal box and some great chalk quarries of the South Downs.*

This page - *Less common than Maunsell freight engines were Lawson Billinton's class K Moguls, arguably the most handsome engines latterly along the South Coast. Those allocated to Fratton shed also worked westwards on to former L&SWR lines. Here at **Fareham**, No. 32337 hauls a long freight off the Eastleigh line, bound for Portsmouth & Southsea. Introduced in 1913, just 17 class K were built for mixed traffic duty. Note the two types of SR three-way starting signals: a balanced bracket on the left; and a theatre-type route indicator on the right beneath a single fluted arm.*

Opposite top - *Humble duty for a mighty beast - Bulleid class Q1 No. 33022 with the pick-up goods near **Bramley**. Never beautiful, seldom clean but always intriguing, 40 of these heavy freight locomotives were built during the 1940s. Working up from Horsham, the Maunsell utility van was delivered to Bramley and the Q1 returned with just the brake. Such light traffic heralded the end of local goods services and the closure of local goods yards. This branch closed in 1965.*

Opposite bottom - *Robert Billinton's class E6 0-6-2 radial tank was one of only two Brighton classes to have remained virtually unchanged during the SR and BR eras. The other was class E5 0-6-2 passenger tank from which the E6 was developed. No. 32417 is seen here with the pick-up goods at **East Dulwich**. Just twelve E6 were built posthumously in 1904-05. No. 417 was one of the final batch which were nameless. Douglas Marsh thereby ended the long tradition of naming every Brighton engine. The turreted building beyond is East Dulwich Hospital.*

*Top - Bulleid Pacifics always looked too big in suburban settings. Approaching **East Croydon** is West Country class No. 34003 Plymouth. It heads an inter-Regional service via the West London line to the South Coast. The GWR commenced regular services from Birkenhead in 1904. A year later, the LN&WR and LB&SCR initiated the Sunny South Special between Liverpool (and other northern towns) and Brighton, Eastbourne and Hastings. During the BR steam era, departure points also included Manchester, Sheffield, Leicester, Walsall, Wolverhampton, High Wycombe, Colne, Loughton, Gidea Park, Poole, Plymouth and Cardiff - some regular and some excursions.*

*Above - **East Croydon** had a curious running arrangement whereby Oxted trains would pass each other on the right. In this picture, Fairburn 2-6-4 tank No. 42090 approaches platform 5 on the Down Local while an Up train departs platform 6. The latter line was bi-directional as far as South Croydon. Precursors of the BR standard class 4MT 2-6-4 tank, this batch of LMS design was built at Brighton, intended to replace the many pre-Grouping locomotives still in service on the Southern. But dieselisation, electrification and line closures overtook the process, making all the classes redundant. These immaculate Bulleid coaches were more pleasurable to ride than their DEMU replacements.*

Oxted's Up advance starter with Maunsell class U1 Mogul No. 31907. By 1961, tender engines were unusual on this line. Introduced in 1928, class U1 was a 3-cylinder version of class U which were rebuilds of the ill-fated River class tanks. The signal is power-operated from the motor (near the base) with a wooden terminal box on the right. The lattice post and finial are early SR, a design inherited from the L&SWR. In this shot, the weighted balance arm is clear, also a steel-wire steadying guy with a chain through the post. There is what looks like a fogman's hut although this is uncommon for a stop signal. Concrete channels on the far side are scattered for impending colour-light signalling.

Top - *A fitted van train enters* **Woldingham** *from the south, headed by Maunsell class W 2-6-4 tank No. 31919. The class was introduced in 1931 for cross-London heavy freight traffic, a development of his 3-cylinder class N1.*

Bottom - *The Oxted line was joint SER/ LB&SCR as far as Crowhurst junction (to the SER's original main line). Propelled by a class H tank, SE&CR push-pull set No. 659 restarts from* **Hurst Green's** *Down home signal. All the conversions to push-pull were made by BR(S).*

Top - *Watering and conversation at* **Oxted** *with standard class 4MT tank No. 80032. The signal box is an LB&SCR type 2c.*

Bottom - *Near* **Edenbridge Town***, class H tank No. 31278 heads an Up push-pull train. Birdcage stock had become rare by 1961.*

Above - Near **Rotherfield**, 36 years after the Grouping, an LB&SCR train in BR(S) livery. The coaches have the distinctive Brighton low arc roof. Class E4 0-6-2 tank No. 32494 was built in 1897 under Robert Billinton as No. 494 Woodgate.

Ancient and modern combinations - *During the late 1950s on the 'Cuckoo' line, the Cole Porter number 'Anything Goes' was an apt description of the vintage trains that carried passengers to and from the South Coast.* **Opposite, top -** *South of* **Mayfield** *on the 'Cuckoo' line, a rich assortment of Brighton and Southern passenger stock, hauled by standard 4MT tank No. 80153, the last but one of its class.*

Opposite, bottom - *Immaculate at* **Eastbourne**, *Maunsell push-pull set 618 with class E4 tank No. 32504. Built in 1900 as No. 504 Chilworth, this village was never served by the LB&SCR but was home in 1961 to Stanley Norris' finescale O gauge model railway, Stroudley & Francisthwaite.*

Left - *BR class 4MT 2-6-4 tank No. 80089 emerges with gusto from* **Oxted** *tunnel in March 1961.*

Bottom - *At* **Ashurst Junction***, Ivatt 2-6-2 tank No. 41260 brings an LMS flavour to services on the Oxted - Tunbridge Wells West line. The branch from East Grinstead comes in from the left.*

Above- Connections at **East Grinstead**. *Fairburn 2-6-4 tank No. 42103 departs with a train to Victoria. An arrival from Victoria is visible below the lower quadrant signal. The right-hand island holds two push-pull trains bound for Three Bridges and Tunbridge Wells West. Passenger access was via staircases from the 'Bluebell' Down platform below.*

Overleaf - *Shunting at* **Grange Road** *with a Bactrian camel - class C2X No. 32535. Robert Billington introduced his 0-6-0 class C2 in 1893 and 55 were built at the Vulcan Foundry. In 1908, spasmodic rebuilding commenced with larger Marsh boilers. No. 521 (opposite) was rebuilt at Brighton in 1925 while No. 535 was rebuilt at Ashford in 1940. The latter also acquired a second dome for a top feed - a provision which was later blanked off.*

Shadows at Eventide

Wainwright and wheelwright, carpenters few; blacksmith and foundryman, riveters too;
To fine railway company workshops they came, 'South Eastern and Chatham' and 'Brighton' by name.
Fifty years on in a Three Bridges bay, their products are worked by the crew of the day,
Filling the water tanks, damping the coal - shadows at eventide, no other soul;
But the ghosts of the craftsmen who moulded this train give joy to the traveller time and again.

Opposite top - *LB&SCR class C2X No. 32521 passes* **St Margarets Junction** *signal box, part of a sequence of manoeuvres to reverse the locomotive. Starting at East Grinstead high level, it had reversed down the spur to the 'Bluebell' line before running forward to here. It will next reverse onto the right-hand curve back to the high level station where it started, but facing the other way. Meanwhile, the signalman has time for a chat with a Permanent Way man.*

Opposite bottom - *Finally, a lament at* **Three Bridges** *for the golden age of steam, featuring Wainwright tank No. 31161, a Brighton push-pull set and a 45 gallon oil drum.*

Permanent Way Notes by Graham Hatton

Further notes on formation work to support the Permanent Way.

The article I wrote in Southern Way No. 8 displayed a few photographs of early track blanketing work taken at Paddock Wood, along with a fairly full description explaining the need for treating poor ground formation. The purpose of this blanketing is to prevent this supporting layer of soil becoming ineffective and leading, through failure, to actual track faults, such as poor top, track twists and accelerated ageing of track components especially the sleepers. Such treatment is known as formation blanketing.

This article adds to the original and shows some more photographs from the same site as well as others to further illustrate an area of track engineering which has been essential in large areas of the Southern Railway, where the ground over which the railway was constructed includes clay. Not all the Southern Railway was so affected, for instance the LSWR enjoyed a lot of good ground formation on its main lines to the South and West. Once clear of the London clay area, long lengths of these lines pass over areas of free draining and firm chalk, as well as gravels, sands and smaller areas of clay. However other lines such as the South Eastern main line through the Weald and on to Hastings, and across from Redhill to Tonbridge suffered from large areas of poor ground formation. The track in these areas often sat directly on the original poor ground in cuttings or in level areas of the country where clay, particularly wet clay, offered poor support here.

When the railways were built the Contractor would use the 'cut and fill' method for construction. The Engineer, in designing the route, would balance the amount of cutting and embankment in the railway's proposed construction, to minimise the cost and the need to import (or remove) large quantities of material over any great distance. Thus what came out of the cuttings went into the nearby embankments, giving rise to the term 'cut and fill'. The Contractor, unless instructed otherwise by the Engineer, used the material to hand, hence so many embankments are built of poor quality material and prone to slumping (sinking).

Over time the poor clay material used in some banks would give rise to major issues for the railway companies to resolve. As with poor formation in cuttings, many of the embankments, although raised above the general poor ground, would still cause severe problems when water eventually percolated into them from the top and caused slippage and slumping in their sides and sometimes top. The difference with embankments is that the railway companies then often added to the problem by adding further material on top to compensate for the loss of the railway's height. Typically porous loco ash was used, as they had plenty of it to dispose of! This further allowed the water to percolate down and pool, deep in the embankment, to worsen further the whole problem of slippage. Many embankments are still affected by poor building material. The immensely wide bank at Sway is a testament to the poor structural ground material used in its construction, Rowborough on the IOW has a mix of material (ash on a clay base) and the embankments south of Tunbridge Wells on the route to Hastings suffer slippage and settlement.

However, returning to the cuttings and low areas of track in this article, the ground formation below the ballast in many cases simply did not have the bearing strength to support a railway as it became affected by rain and vertical pumping by trains passing. This was less obvious in the early days, but as train weights and speeds increased, the impact and direct loading on the underlying ground formation, through the often thin layer of ballast, increased and the wet clay would ooze up through the ballast and around the sleepers as the result of the pumping action of passing trains. The ballast would become heavily contaminated and unable to fulfil the main requirements of free drainage and support to the track.

Where large areas of the ground were composed of clay, what the best the railway companies did, and still continue to do, is to form a flexible cap on top of the clay to try to stop migration of the clay particles into the ballast layer and spread the load from increasing train weights more evenly over the available formation and thus reduce the load per square area known as the bearing pressure. Such a treatment has to be flexible as the ground settles unevenly, whilst the avoidance of cracks in this capping layer is important.

Modern methods use geo-textile woven material with plastic grids for added strength, but traditionally sand was and still is used to form a semi flexible dense layer on top of the clay, though nowadays it is also to protect the geo textile material from puncture by sharper stones.

The following are therefore an additional selection of historic pictures from various sites on the Southern to illustrate further this complex and often messy activity.

Opposite - Paddock Wood Station, November 1947, showing the tracked facing shovel excavator in use (taken from the other direction to that in Southern Way No.8). Clearly all it had so far dug out did not fit in the solitary wagon! A full train of wagons must have been used, but this may have been being changed over at the time of this photograph and a single wagon left to allow the work to slowly continue until the next train arrived: though at this stage the machine appears to have been stopped as the wagon is full and there is nobody now in this area. The gang behind are spreading the sand which would have been pushed and shovelled out of wagons to actually 'blind out' or blanket the clay sub soil formation after the deep dig had removed the heavily contaminated ballast. The dig needed to be deep enough to get a good depth of sand below the new ballast without raising the track level, which in turn might affect clearances to over-bridges. Often about 6-9 inches of sand was used, but greater depths, as here, are not uncommon. Thus blanketing has always been a slower activity than, say, ballast cleaning due to the greater volume of material to be removed and replaced. Normal service appears to have been carried on around this site with a local train in the up platform.

Opposite top - *It may be a black and white photo, but this shows the sort of underlying clay so typical of blanketing sites. Looking carefully, the exposed ends of the adjacent Up Main show about nine inches of reasonable ballast, but a further 18 to 24 inches of largely clay have been removed before sand has been added at the far end of this cut: under the small group of men seen there. As can be appreciated, working on blanketing sites was definitely not a task for wearing good clothing, anywhere near the clay it was wet, it would stick to anything! Also of note on the Up Slow platform, is the vast amount of merchandise so typically moved by train before the industry largely lost this role to road transport. Note: Referring back to the earlier item in Southern Way No 8, are further views of the formation and the small face shovel used to remove the soiled material, are shown for the same site.*

Opposite bottom - *This and the next two pictures were taken at Penge, under the flyover of the line to Crystal Palace, in November 1948. The sand for the blinding layer is being dropped from the side door flap of the wagon on the right. The flap is actually being propped by a length of wood to try and shoot the ballast further out into the hole and not drop under the wagon wheels of the adjacent track on which the wagon stands. The photograph shows both company and private owner wagons used for this task, specialist wagons did exist, but a lot of use was made of old wagons which were in reasonable supply at the time. Also of note is the man clinging precariously to the left hand wagon and probably pulling the sand out with a shovel. The men in the hole are simply shovelling the sand round and roughly levelling it.*

Above - *A wonderful mix of adapted plant, old wagons and sheer physical work is shown in this photograph, though there seem a lot of spectators as well. The face shovel excavator seems to be leaning over in this view so presumably this is to provide a cross fall or grade to a drain to remove ground water. In this case, as the machine could only dig a level base relative to itself; one caterpillar track might be raised on material or old sleepers to allow the machine simply to dig at an angle. Its use here is in the loading of wagons with spoil. The action of its bucket, which could not be reversed, is the wrong way round to assist unloading of material. The generator seems to have been adapted to run on railway wheels, though how this and the excavator got to site is unclear. Presumably the generator is providing compressed air to a pneumatic breaker used to break up harder areas of the ballast prior to loading, rather than using pick axes. The contaminated ballast might be poor at support as it tended to ooze out around the sleepers, but it could be like breaking up toffee to remove. Sometimes wagons were unloaded of sand before being reloaded with contaminated ballast, though in time segregation of activities became the norm to avoid contamination of new material, particularly when wagons were only partly emptied before reloading!*

Sand was usually used, though this material looks more coarse, so perhaps grit was being trialled instead, and hence some of the spectators and the photographs.

This is a Delmag Frog Rammer, and according to the back of the photograph it is called 'Barco Tamping'. The rammer vibrates using an inbuilt engine and is angled to assist it to move forward. It was probably very noisy in use and the cause of excessive vibration to the operator. The main point of the activity is to compact the sand / grit to form a dense layer of material. Loose sand, as found on the beach, is of no real value, the material (normally quarried green sand) has to be compacted, though by the nature of sand it retains the ability to slightly flex and reseal when loaded to maintain the blanket quality required of it.

Clearly other trials were undertaken at this time to try to form a guaranteed impermeable layer below the track ballast. This and the view opposite were taken at Clapham Junction, though not on the same site or track. They show the use of pre formed concrete panels laid out on top of the poor formation which has already been blinded, or partly blanketed, with compacted sand. The frame or trammel on the left has been used to get a constant bed level using the adjacent sleepers as a guide, prior to laying the slabs. The rail crane has been brought to the end of the track and is lifting the slabs from the wagons to the pre formed base prior to covering with further sand and then ballast. Finally another panel of track can be added to the track the crane is stood on, the crane can then move forward and repeat the process. Note the 'rail slippers' on the very end of the rail, used to form stops and prevent the crane running off the rail end. The crane driver would otherwise find it very difficult to see the end of the rail. Again a wonderful collection of old wagons has been pressed into service for this task.

Opposite page - This shows the slabs better, the site is possibly on the Up Southampton main line under Battersea Rise Bridge. The tops of the slabs clearly slope to the left to allow proper drainage and they are again bedded on sand, but this time ballast is being directly loaded on to them from the grab bucket excavator, though it is not entirely clear where the ballast came from! The concrete slabs appear to have separately fitted containment curbs fitted on the low side, but maybe they were also intended to fit on the higher, right side. Judging by the looks on the faces of the P.Way staff, they were not used to ballast delivered this way, but were probably jolly pleased it didn't involve much shovelling, still the norm for many activities at this time. I have worked in this area and the formation is often very wet clay resulting in poor bearing strength, but I have not yet encountered a concrete base, which would be interesting. So perhaps the trial was not a success.

Until recently, after all the track had been blanketed, the ballast spread and the track replaced, the time honoured method of unloading top stone (the stone to fill in around the sleepers and form a ballast shoulder) was using hopper wagons. The SR owned Meldon Quarry, from which was available a particularly hard granite, very suitable for ballast. It also produced as a side product, a dust from the stone, always referred to as 'Meldon Dust', ideal for blanketing and also pathways, and in time forming a layer almost as hard as a road surface. To get the ballast to sites all over the SR, the company built bogie hopper wagons (as its predecessor the LSWR did, and possibly one of these is shown behind the first hopper). These were built to cover the repetitive mileage at good speed to Meldon, which is to the west of Okehampton in Devon. The wagons were returned to 'collection sidings' to form full trains back to the quarry. This was a journey they made every week wherever they had been used over the whole region. These wagons had a central divide, so they were actually two hoppers and were fitted with three bottom doors to each of the hoppers operated by the wheels on the wagon ends. Two doors led to the side shoots and one door unloaded in the middle of the track. The bigger bogie hoppers had the advantage of the operator being able to open and close the ballast doors, so if the train stopped you could close them again before a mountain of ballast was dropped. It also meant you could trickle ballast out more easily to where it was actually wanted. The four wheel hoppers' doors were arranged differently and opening them was more of a commitment. The smaller hoppers also tended to 'ride up' on the ballast if it got under the wheels, particularly as they became lighter when empty, with the possibility of derailing these lighter wagons; the 'bigger brother' hoppers crushed a lot more of it. Care also had to be taken to make sure the doors were closed when the wagons left site empty and any displaced ballast was cleared from any ledge from which it could fall from a moving wagon, which might have been travelling at some speed. The job of unloading ballast was a task requiring direction from one man on the ground to coordinate the train driver and the men who opened the hopper doors, and was a lot easier in daylight. Before the continuous lighting of sites became more normal, unloading ballast at night by lamplight was difficult. Excess ballast and ballast in the wrong place was a distinct possibility and then without a plough van, a vehicle used less on the Southern than elsewhere, it was a case of shovelling the excess stone around before restoring train services, an unpopular job and something traditionally meted out to those who had been responsible for putting the ballast in the wrong place.

COLOUR INTERLUDE

A wonderfully atmospheric image taken at 10.00 pm one night on platform 8 at Guildford. Q1 No. 33001 waiting to go on shed sometime in the early 1960s.

Viv Orchard

The views on these two and the last page are six uncaptioned colour slides that came into my possession recently. They are almost certainly taken in the mid-fifties and show scenes now gone forever.

On these two pages are five pictures in and from Bricklayers Arms Junction box. This was a B.R. (S.R) Type 15 box opened on 8 October 1950 and equipped with a Westinghouse 'L' type miniature lever frame (No 118) of 55 levers. It closed on 20 July 1975, the area subsequently being controlled from London Bridge Panel.

Photos 1, 2, and 3 show the interior of the box and are taken at about 10.50, according to the clock, with the signalman and box boy in the appropriate dress of the period. There is also another visitor to the box in addition to the photographer and there are sandwiches on the table. Is this some organised visit, and does anyone know the identity of the signalman and box boy?

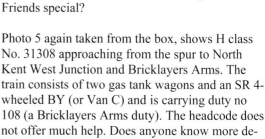

Photo 4 is of up train headed by an ex SECR 4-4-0 probably an L1, again taken from the box. The fact that the factory clock shows 7.45 and the sun is very far round in the west means that this must be summer. The train carries a headboard but it's not clear enough to read. Could it be a Hop Pickers Friends special?

Photo 5 again taken from the box, shows H class No. 31308 approaching from the spur to North Kent West Junction and Bricklayers Arms. The train consists of two gas tank wagons and an SR 4-wheeled BY (or Van C) and is carrying duty no 108 (a Bricklayers Arms duty). The headcode does not offer much help. Does anyone know more details of the working?

I am indebted to Martin Elms for identifying the location and for box and train information.

Colour photos Terry Cole Collection

We go across the water for Photo 6 which is taken at Ryde St. Johns Rd. It's a lovely picture even if posed. But who are the pupils, they must be in their sixties by now/ The coach is equally intriguing. It appears to be one of the two LCDR Full Brakes No. 1011 or 1012. Certainly the arc roof and the door layout match. No. 1011, which was fully clad in steel sheet in the 1930s, was withdrawn in March 1957 and No. 1012, which retained its panelling later, was withdrawn in April. Scrapping at this period usually took place at St Helens rather than in the cramped yard at Ryde Works so maybe this careful dismantling is so that parts could be used for their replacement full brakes which were being converted at the works from SECR 4-compartment brakes. However, Nos. 1013 / 14 / 15 were converted in late 1956 and only No. 1016 converted as late as April 19 57. Any additional information welcome. My thanks to David Wigley for his identification of the location and thoughts on the coach.